Praise for *Becoming a Sage*

"There is really nothing I can write to convey how much Sharon has influenced my life and helped my family. She is one of those rare and precious teachers who understands that having 'a life well lived' requires that we first nurture our own clarity, artfulness, grace, humor, and compassion and then stand ready to serve others by lifting them up with what we have learned."

—**Peter Alsop,** educator, musician, and songwriter/performer

"For a long time, I've paid attention to the wise people I've encountered. Not only are they wonderful teachers (whether they know it or not), they are obviously people who have been paying attention to their own lives and the lessons along the way.

"Happily, Sharon Cruse is one of these wise women who has always been willing to pass along her personal lessons to those of us who want to live richer, smoother, healthier, happier lives. Pay attention to her and you'll discover what I mean."

—**Barbara Winter,** author of *Making a Living Without a Job*,
self-employment advocate

"As a man who has lived through many tough life lessons and has shared a close personal and professional relationship with Sharon for the past thirty years, I can confidently say that Sharon is a person gifted with an ability to heal others through her words—words that have been formed through many, many years of accumulated life knowledge and experience. These two things create wisdom. Sharon has turned her wisdom into healing power that has made her a much-revered sage amongst sages. If you are seeking life wisdom, I strongly suggest you read this book."

—**Robert Subby,** psychologist and author of
Healing the Family Within and *Lost in the Shuffle*

"I first met Sharon Cruse thirty years ago and have been blessed and enlightened by her compassion and wisdom. We all have a life pilgrimage and Sharon lovingly shared hers in the work that she does. With her wisdom and loving heart, she has encouraged and guided many people who are seeking assistance and direction in their own personal life pilgrimages. Sharon is one of the gentle and wise people on the planet."

—**Harry Owens Jr., MD, MIM,** volunteer doctor in underserved areas
of the world for Project HOPE, Continuing Promise,
Project Medishare, and Lifeline Christian Mission

"Sharon Wegscheider-Cruse has been a life-altering influence for so many people, including me. I first met Sharon in my mother's living room, thirty-six years ago, when she was doing a weekend of work with my family of origin. After that weekend, I felt a burden lift from my shoulders and it was the beginning of what I would now call recovery from the childhood trauma I experienced growing up with parental addiction. I felt that I was seeing behind a screen, into the back stage of addiction, with insight to what we now call ACoA issues; at that time all of this went unnamed and was often times invisible. Sharon was instrumental in making that experience visible. Along with making it safe to surface, she helped to open up great inner surges toward healing, happiness, and celebration—and towards taking charge of my life. Sharon had a vision and the courage to actualize it. She lit a path for others to follow. She lit a path for me."

—**Tian Dayton, PhD, TEP,** author of numerous books
including *Neuropsychodrama and the Treatment of Relational Trauma,*
Forgiving and Moving On, Emotional Sobriety, and
The ACoA Trauma Syndrome

"Courageous, transparent, and insightful. Here is a memoir of a different and delightful sort. From an early onset storyteller through challenges, successes, and failures, Sharon emerges as an elder who is aging consciously and positively—an authentic sage. Reading Sharon's memoir is like sitting with her, sipping tea, and being in the presence of incarnate wisdom and inspiration."

—**Jack Williamson,** chaplain, colonel, USAF (Ret)
co-facilitator, Boulder, Colorado, chapter of Sage-ing International

"SAGE is an attribute that Sharon exemplifies. She is Sincere about helping others find their way. Ageless in that she embraces all stages of life and makes the most of each day. She is Generous with her time and energy, building others to find their true self while Encouraging all of us to follow our separate paths."

—**Cheryl Keller,** RN, program director, group facilitator

"Sharon Wegscheider-Cruse has reached beyond her role as a mentor and pioneer in codependency treatment and recovery. With the humility and wisdom of a true sage, Sharon shares with us deeply personal stories to uncover meaning, wisdom, and clarity, transforming our fears and misgivings about aging into excited anticipation and empowerment. She saves us from the stereotypes of the past to discover the beauty, wisdom, and resilience that come with age. For all who anticipate the role of the sage, this book is our guide.

"Sharon is one of the angels in my life, having first helped guide me in my own journey of recovery and into my role mentoring others. She continues to be a beloved friend, lighting up my life and becoming part of my family constellation. I am blessed to have her with me on my journey in life and honored to be part of hers."

—Cynthia A. Taylor, MD, life fellow, American Psychiatric Association, founder, Integrative Psychiatry, LLC

BECOMING A SAGE

Discovering Life's Lessons, One Story at a Time

SHARON WEGSCHEIDER-CRUSE

Health Communications, Inc.
Deerfield Beach, Florida

www.hcibooks.com

Library of Congress Cataloging-in-Publication Data
is available through the Library of Congress

© 2016 Sharon Wegscheider-Cruse

ISBN-13: 978-07573-1904-4 (Paperback)
ISBN-10: 07573-1904-1 (Paperback)
ISBN-13: 978-07573-1905-1 (ePub)
ISBN-10: 07573-1905-X (ePub)

Publisher: Health Communications, Inc.
        3201 S.W. 15th Street
        Deerfield Beach, FL 33442–8190

Cover design by Lawna Patterson Oldfield
Interior design and formatting by Lawna Patterson Oldfield

I dedicate this book to my children,
Patrick, Sandra, and Deborah,
who walked with me in all the early years and
waited for me to grow up with them; to my
soul mate, Joe, who came into my life over thirty years ago
and showed me what a coupleship is all about;
and to my grandchildren, Matthew, Melanie,
Christopher, Cheyenne, Ryan, Sierra, and Andrew,
who, along with my children, are my harvest.
God bless them all.

About the Cover

On my daily walk, I see this tree. It impresses me with its deep roots while still reaching toward the sky and stars. It changes colors each year on its journey—much like the life of a sage.

CONTENTS

Chapter Seven: LAS VEGAS

Chapter Eight: FROM RESTLESS SEEKER TO SAGE

PART TWO

Chapter Nine: WHAT IS A SAGE?

ACKNOWLEDGMENTS

Thank you one more time to Peter Vegso and Gary Seidler for their belief in me and their interest in my books. It's been an honor to have worked with them for the past thirty-seven years. Right along with them, there have been two people who have made it possible for this book to take shape: my soul mate Joe Cruse, and my son and personal help-desk Patrick Egan. I thank both of them personally and professionally for their teaching, their support, and their technology help in more ways than can be listed. The hours of sitting at my computer made the birthing of this book and idea a reality. A special thanks to Patrick Cotter, who helps me take my ideas and formulate them, all while providing me with laughter and insight. Peg Musegades was there with her creative artwork that brings the pages to vision when needed. Thank you Peg. Once the book goes to Health Communications, thanks to Lawna Oldfield for her work on designing the cover to reflect a special tree that I walk by daily and for the beautiful inside design. Finally, I have been blessed by having Christine Belleris keep me informed, give feedback, and reshape my writing to make it work for the reader. She has been wonderful to work with.

FOREWORD

My very dear friend Sharon is one of those blessed people who has the grace of gratitude for all the many challenges she has faced in life. Growing up in a family affected by the trauma and dysfunction of two alcoholic parents set her on a remarkable life journey that has seen her become one of the preeminent pioneers of the recovery movement in America, and across the world today.

Her own healing journey began when she sought treatment for herself as a non-addict adult child of alcoholics at a time when there was very little known about the impact of addiction on the families of addicts. Incredibly, she put herself through a residential treatment program for alcoholics, where she found the inspiration to begin her tireless work in developing and shaping the specialized field of treatment for families affected by addiction.

I first knew Sharon through her book *Another Chance: Hope and Health for the Alcoholic Family*, which changed my life with its insights about the disease of addiction and led to our meeting in 1990 while she was in Australia on a book tour. In a moment of courage and connection with my higher power I invited this intriguing woman home for an Aussie barbecue with my family. To my shock and delight she came. Looking out over Sydney Harbor, laughing with Sharon over her poignant stories of chaos and healing, I envied her wisdom and knew that I had found a guide and mentor to show me the way to heal my life. I was intensely curious to understand how she had overcome the challenges, the pain, and the craziness of life in an alcoholic family, and had gone on to create a life so filled with spirituality. Sharon had found the purpose, meaning, connection, and joy of a life well lived, and I yearned for the same.

Since then, Sharon has had a profound influence on my life professionally and personally, as a mentor and as a friend. I, too, was the adult child of two alcoholics, we are the same age, and I, too, have focused my professional life on endeavoring to bring healing to addicts and their families at my treatment center, South Pacific Private (SPP), in Sydney, Australia. Our friendship has flourished across the hemispheres as she travelled down under to present and consult at SPP, and I travelled regularly to the United States for professional inspiration.

Sharon has worked collaboratively and creatively alongside many clinicians and healers that have been at the forefront of the recovery movement, including her partner of thirty years, Dr. Joe Cruse, the founding medical director of the Betty Ford Center. Sharon brought new ways of thinking about the process of healing and has created a platform of knowledge, expertise, and understanding that underpins all the most effective family treatment programs available today. Sharon was the founding chairperson of the National Association for Children of Alcoholics (NACoA), an organization that now has chapters all around the world.

My most precious times with Sharon over the last decade have been our yearly retreat in Arizona with a special group of wise woman, where she guides and challenges us to grow through reflection, connection, sharing, and healing.

This book is for all the people out there who yearn to make a difference in our world. It is for those who have suffered, for those searching for answers, for those seeking wisdom, and for those who just love a good read about a remarkable life.

Sharon passionately loves the creative journey of healing through self-discovery, and in this book she shares her own very personal story in a way that inspires readers to aspire to greater possibilities for their own life.

Sharon is truly a sage: a person of profound wisdom. She is a woman who has followed an inner calling, and with this book she is honoring her place among the great sages of our time in sharing her wisdom with us all.

—**Lorraine Wood**
author, cofounder, and executive director,
South Pacific Private Hospital, Sydney, Australia

INTRODUCTION

Sages are people who have reached a time of inner [...] yet yearn for more. The art of becoming a sage mixes p[...] with learning from ancient and historical people who h[...] own wisdom. Sages know that they stand on the shoulders of those who have gone before. When ancient wisdom and current wisdom collide, they activate the process of becoming a living sage.

Sages are radiant, vital, grateful, curious, settled, accepting, and responsible. They are mystics, psychics, shamans, and wise men and women. By their very presence, they lay down paths and lead others to find their own path. Gurus encourage people to follow their teachings; sages encourage others to find their own personal path.

Historian and author Tamara Hareven identifies "time" as a life span, an approach that helps us to see the developmental transitions and changes that are the defining moments in our lives. Some of these moments we choose and others are thrust upon us, testing our resiliency. Sages are the mentors, leaders, and teachers who honor our stories that have shaped us and then help pass them on to the people of the future. Our memories are transmitted in words, traditions, and wisdom.

Writing this book at this time is recapturing and sharing my memories one more time. We live in a culture and era where many things have been kept private and unspoken. For me, this is the time to tell some stories for the first time and retell others that are important. It's not always easy to tell our stories; it can be too scary and too private. As we grow older, however, we find courage and confidence by deciding to become "a teller of truth." We have earned that position, and we gain mastery as we tell our stories. Each of us has a first and last day of life. In between, each of us has an incredible number of stories. Our stories are the legacy that we leave to family and friends.

Dr. Tim Frank, a compassionate sage, once whispered in my ear, "Keep the wisdom; let the experience go." Little did he know the profound effect those words would have on me. He awakened in me the acceptance that I have lived that "letting go" process for a very long time. When I failed to heed those words, life became a painful struggle. My life has had soaring highs and deep lows. It has been a journey of "lessons learned" and a celebration of living with those lessons. My hope is that my stories will bring you some solace, comfort, and joy—and inspire you to write or record your own stories.

Once a great lesson has been learned, Dr. Frank explained, there is no going back. The butterfly never returns to the cocoon. In my programs of recovery in the Black Hills, I used to say, "Once you know, you cannot 'not know' again. Information must lead to change or it becomes depression."

Peter, Gary, and Dan

My life has been graced with many sages, female and male. In my family, strength, intellect, and goodness came through many powerful women; male energy, however, was glaringly absent. But the universe did provide me with masterful and loving male sages that have led me to a very balanced and rich adulthood that continues to this day.

Two special male sages, Peter Vegso and Gary Seidler, became my publishers. They, like other men before them, believed in me, and my talents. Peter and Gary moved to the United States from Canada with dreams and talents of their own. One of the gifts they both possess is an inner goodness that helped them discover the value of respect and relationships in both their personal and professional lives.

For me, there was no sharp distinction between being friends and coworkers. Professional distance was neither part of my training nor my value system. Meeting Peter and Gary was life-changing and affirming.

Colorado Opportunity

My first connection with them is a story on its own, and this book is told in a storytelling style because basically, I am a storyteller. When we met, I was a counselor and was setting up a practice in Minnesota to work with youth and adult children of alcoholics. Speaking in workshops and traveling for the agency that hired me had been the extent of lecturing that I had done, even though public speaking had come naturally to me ever since high school.

A telephone call brought an amazing invitation one day. Virginia Satir, a master family therapist well known in the field, was scheduled to deliver the keynote address at a major national conference in Colorado. Her topic was family therapy; hundreds were expected to attend. Virginia had fallen ill at the last minute and suggested that I replace her. I had about two days to prepare and get to Colorado. Without hesitation, I accepted. I was soon to meet Dan Bartmettler, another wonderful sage.

From Local Speaker to National Stage

The success of that conference is what brought me to the attention of Gary Seidler and Peter Vegso. They then invited me to speak at one of their conferences. These three dynamic men formed much of my professional male interaction for many years.

They helped me by putting me on several national stages. They also showed me what a team of healthy men running healthy organizations looked like. They built a field of addiction, family, and codependency knowledge that had not existed before. Their conferences, the books they published, and the workshops they staged have saved and enriched the lives of countless people. The training they developed has produced competent therapists and innovative leaders in the fields of addiction, codependency, and mental health. I am humbled to have been part of the birth of a movement and development of a field.

Storytelling as an Art

I can't help being a storyteller. Life reveals itself to me and directs me through stories. When someone brings up a topic, I think, *I have a story about that*. The stories just flow out of me. Once one of my children said, "Mom, you tell too many stories." Then she added, "You also sometimes embellish those stories and they are not exactly the way I remember it."

I took that to heart and thought about it. I decided that being a storyteller is just who I am, embellishments and all. I hope my stories will mostly be a source of joy to me and of interest to others. I do add texture, color, and details. Hemingway once said, "All good books are alike in that they are truer than if they had really happened." As long as they are true, the details can afford to be rich and colorful.

I love this quote from Madeleine L'Engle: "Stories make us more alive, more human, courageous, and loving." When I tell a story, it will contain many facts, and it will also contain my memory of an incident that is true for me. Others might have different memories. I will be sharing many stories from the people who have enriched my life. They are ordinary people doing extraordinary things.

As this book took shape, it became clear to me that a pure memory is only pure when you are asleep or in a coma. Otherwise we are changing every single time we remember something, maybe changing every hour and every day. My rewrites have been persistent and plentiful. Each time we remember, we remember differently because *we* are different. It has been hard work to freeze-frame life, story by story, to capture the memories that have made me who I am today.

Some of my journey is heavy, some is light, some is dark, and some is full of joy. Understanding my life has become increasingly focused, serene, and empowering. I have been able to understand the stages that defined me inward and outward. Going deep inside to find my shadows and bringing them forward to take their place beside my gifts was a brutally honest journey. It has brought me inspiration, inner peace, and personal power. As Joan Didion said, "We tell ourselves stories in order to live life."

I invite you to share my journey through storytelling with Carl Jung's words in mind: "Who looks outside, dreams; who looks inside, awakens." Each story calls to us and presents a karmic lesson. The word *karma* will be used often in this book; the definition I refer to is "a person's actions in this world that help decide their fate in future times." The action can be words spoken or deeds done. It is the principle of causality, which holds that an individual's intent and action influence his or her future. There are many schools of thought about, and definitions of, this principle, but this is the one I will be referring to in my writings about karma.

Sometimes people are stuck in their lives and cannot get past certain situations. I hold that when someone stays stuck too long, he or she may be doing someone else's work. Each of us has a karmic ancestry; it's import. that we separate from it so we can move on. Sometimes we have to leave a situation and accept that it is not ours to solve. It belonged to our ancestry and we have just carried it.

Becoming a sage is not defined by age. Each life is lived individually. Not everyone lives through all the natural cycles. Some lives are shorter, and some manage to live through all the cycles in that shorter life span. Some people advance in years but never make it through all the cycles. My plan is to go through each of the cycles and transformations and let you decide where you are and where you might like to go in your journey.

I believe in stories, in their ability to keep the dead alive and the living engaged. There are no rules in storytelling; your story is your truth.

To have known the extremes of joy, grief, loss, birth, letting go, poverty, wealth, fame, rejection, comfort, and fear is to be fully aware of one's self. When all the ingredients come together in a recipe of life, we become a personal masterpiece. The sweet and the sour blend in the production of each life. So it is. We are the sum of our experiences and choices.

For me, the decision to tell my story at this time, both personally and professionally, is because I accept myself as a link in a chain. The intensity of my relationships with people who have gone before me needs to be linked to those who come after me. I hold stories that no one else knows and it's time to tell them.

Even though my name has been before the public for forty-three years through my books, movies, workshops, and lectures, my private life has been private. That was always my choice because I believed that my soul mate, my children, and my grandchildren deserved autonomy. They have their own views and their own stories.

I want to be clear that I love them all with my whole heart and soul; they are the most important people in the world to me. They will only be mentioned indirectly throughout, unless it's integral to a certain story. I have tried to keep it my story and not their story. Hopefully, some day they will each write their own story. My story is mine to share and these are the reasons for choosing now as the right time. I choose:

ɛr retreat

ure

ɛ retirement

* Joy over depression
* Small over big
* Manageability over overwhelm
* Curiosity over "been there, done that"
* Learning over knowing

As Robert Browning wrote, "Grow old along with me!/The best is yet to be." I invite you to share my journey and my stories.

The first eight chapters of this book comprise Part One. It focuses on telling some of my stories and inviting you to share in the life lessons that have brought me to this time. A reflection that sums up the lesson learned follows each story. As a therapist, public speaker, entrepreneur, and author, I've already told many of these stories. They cover so many extraordinary experiences and events and hold so many lessons. I love telling them.

Sharon Wegscheider-Cruse

PART ONE

"After nourishment,
shelter and companionship,
stories are the thing we need
most in the world."

—Philip Pullman

Chapter One

THE EARLY YEARS

My Restless Soul

"The longest journey is the journey inward,
for he who has chosen his destiny has started upon
his quest for the source of his being."
—Dag Hammarskjöld

Bob Subby is one of my favorite sages. For years, I have sought his words and his guidance. It felt strange the first time I called him—he was so much younger than me. How could he help me with issues connected to getting older and with so many unexpected changes? Yet my intuition said he was the right person. He would understand and advise.

In telling my story, there were tears, questions, confusion, and a sense of real sadness. When I finished, he simply said, "You are not satisfied chewing your cud." That's all. The simple statement brought my tears to a sudden stop, and piqued my curiosity. Then he told me "Cows chew their cud," and explained and I felt better. He was right and there was nothing wrong with me. I just didn't like "chewing my cud." I always wanted more than that. I made some very important decisions that day and haven't chewed cud since.

Cud and Cows Are Important

Whenever you see a cow, it tends to be chewing. Cows have to chew their food twice or more to digest it. They spend at least eight hours a day just chewing their cud. Their normal chewing and cud chewing requires about 40,000 jaw movements a day. The whole process of a cow's four stomachs needing to add their part to the cud is not important to the story. Suffice it to say that eventually what their stomachs produce is called cud. One could argue that this is a boring point and an unimportant piece of information. Trust me, I am going someplace with it. While that is all that the cow does for its lifetime, it is an important function.

From cows come the world's supply of milk, cream, and butter. And when the cow is through producing those products, and makes more baby cows to add to the food supply, it's often slaughtered to provide steaks, hamburgers, and roast beef. A cow can provide up to 500 pounds of beef. And then there are the byproducts that include medicinal drugs such as insulin. It takes the pancreases from twenty-six cattle to provide enough insulin to keep one diabetic person alive for one year. Then there are the surgical sutures, chewing gum, gelatin from bones, and sausage casings. The list goes on: leather, insulation, oils and lubricants, detergents, piano keys, wallpaper, and more. And all cows do is chew their cud. They have an important mission and they are satisfied with that.

Humans, Satisfied, and Restless

Bob then observed that humans are the same way. Most people are satisfied to do their jobs and complete their missions. They go to school, get their certifications and degrees, eat in restaurants, marry or stay single, and sometimes they become parents. They shop, drive cars, go to ballgames, and they watch TV. These are the things expected of them and they do them. It is what makes the world go around. There are millions of wonderful people doing their job and fulfilling expectations. It's a form of chewing cud. They do it over and over without much thought. It's simple, but important.

Then there are the restless souls. They are always not quite satisfied. There is something more that they want; sometimes it's defined, sometimes it's not. Sometimes they do not do what others want them to do or expect from them. From time to time, their souls cry out for more understanding, a new project, a vision to manifest, something to be created, something to be improved upon. Both missions are important to fulfill in this world. I just happen to be one of the latter. Creating is an outlet for my restless soul and when I create, I feel fulfilled. When I understood that it's okay to "chew your cud" and be satisfied, and that it's also okay to be restless, it made sense. Restlessness is a gift—it signals that there is more to come.

Maya Angelou expressed it this way: "Most people don't grow up. Most people age. They find parking places, honor their credit cards, get married, have children, and call that maturity. What that is, is aging."

LESSONS LEARNED

We cannot judge each other on our approach to life. It's a fine endeavor to carry on tradition and the way things have been throughout tradition. It is also a fine endeavor to want to change, to discover that which has not been done before. Restlessness could be a form of creativity. We need both approaches to keep order and create evolution. We all need each other.

The Hobos

"Know who you are and where you came from.
Embrace yourself."

—Maya Angelou

My soul was restless very early on. My birth took place in a rock quarry town called Jasper in southern Minnesota. The town was named for the quarry, one of the world's largest quartzite quarries. The rock, jasper, is used in jewelry, construction, cemetery headstones, and has countless other applications. Jasper is beautiful raw and polished. The quarry has been operating for more than eighty years and extends almost a mile underground; there is still a great deal of rock left to be quarried. My ancestors from Scotland developed the quarry. I spent my first years in Jasper during the Great Depression.

My grandmother managed and cooked in a little town three miles away called Ihlen. Trains on the Great Northern Railroad stopped there for food and passengers. The trains often stopped in Jasper as well and became an important part of my early growing-up years.

In my home and among my extended family, we were taught to share whatever we have at all times. Everyone in my family was generous. We lived in each other's homes, and my grandma adopted two parentless children at a time when she had very little.

In the nineteen-thirties and forties, hobos were very common. Many men did not have work and rode the rails looking to pick up jobs. My grandma was a great cook and her food today would be considered upscale bistro. On the back porch, Grandma had a wicker basket and the locals would put in worn, clean clothes they discarded.

Sometimes there would be blankets they no longer used. Hobos would come by and pick them up. Each morning she would put out homemade bread and a kettle of soup on a hot plate burner. Hobos finally marked her porch with the sign of safety in hobo language, indicating that this was a safe house.

I liked to visit with them and sometimes one of them would take me for a walk around town. I was proud to meet them and hear their great adventure stories. They made me want more, to see what they had seen and experienced.

That's when I started running away; I ran away from the ages of five to eight. Sometimes I went into the country and explored the big concrete vaults that ran under country roads; other times I went to the cemetery about three miles from town and practiced reading names on the tombstones. Sometimes I would lie and tell a hobo or engineer that I was supposed to go see a relative in a different town. I'd ask if I could ride in the boxcar with the hobos or with the engineer up front. It was more like I was running to something and less like I was running from anything. I was never afraid and never hurt. Even then my soul was restless for something more.

Once while in high school, I was in a neighboring town riding on a homecoming float. As the float went by the grandstand, my name and a bit about me was read over the loudspeaker. An old man from the bleachers came over to me as I got off the float and told me that he remembered me: he was one of my grandma's hobos. That was sweet.

LESSONS LEARNED

What I learned from the hobos was that one should never judge people by their outsides. Sometimes people would tell me to stay away from them because they might be dirty. Yet they were wonderful to me. They explained trains, took me on walks, and told me funny stories.

Chicken Sexing

*"As a freshman in college, I was having a lot of
trouble adjusting. I took a meditation class to handle anxiety.
It really helped. Then as a grad student at Harvard, I was awarded
a predoctoral traveling fellowship to India, where my
focus was on the ancient systems of psychology
and meditation practices of Asia."*

—Daniel Goleman

Oscar Wilde once said, "The things worth learning can't be taught." They are mentored shown and experienced. They are intuitive.

I grew up with chicken sexers so I thought everybody knew about them. Every Monday morning at 4 AM from May through October, they came to our town. My dad owned a hatchery and hatched ten incubators of baby chickens on Monday mornings in season. The count was a few thousand a hatch.

Sexing chickens was a skill the Japanese had developed and delivered as a service. The purpose of sexing is to separate females (for their egg-producing qualities) from the males, which were then culled from the group. The males had little value except for food consumption. My dad and I would go to the hatchery early in the dark mornings and set up the sexing operation. We would place coffee cans on a long table and watch for the big car with four men to arrive at the hatchery. Only one spoke English and he and my dad would converse.

Then the work began. For four hours, until our business opened for the day, the men would pick up a newborn chick in each hand and squeeze a fluid present in them right after birth. By observing the fluid, they could tell if they were roosters or hens and divide them in boxes accordingly. This is important work, as the hens had high value and the roosters very little. I thought the sexers were magical. Today however, sexing is a dying art, and there are fewer schools and training programs in Japan. To my knowledge, all chicken sexers are still Japanese.

We would keep one rooster for every twenty-five hens. The hens were put in boxes and my dad and I would count them every Monday evening. There were hundreds of them. My dad would give as many roosters as they wanted to any farmers who wanted to raise them for food. Still there were hundreds that had to be destroyed and that process scared and saddened me. He also kept about fifty in the spring, which he would dip in food dye and put them in the picture window of his business so all the kids in town could come see them and visit them. My dad would give the roosters to any kids who wanted them. Many a farmer was reluctant to butcher a chicken with colored feather tips once it had become a family pet.

My dad and I would work on Monday nights sorting the baby chicks into a hundred per box, twenty-five to a square. We would pick them up and count them by hand as we listened to the *Lux Radio Theatre*. The soap maker sponsored the show. I still remember these one-hour sessions on Monday night after all these years. Most people like to have a special memory of their dad; this is mine.

LESSONS LEARNED

I was influenced by the Japanese chicken sexers. They were smart, funny, and looked and talked differently from the people I had known up until then. They always brought me a gift and made my dad happy as they worked with our chickens. I learned to respect and trust people who were different from me.

Pheasant Hunting

"The important thing is not to stop questioning.
Curiosity has its own reason for existing."
—Albert Einstein

My hometown, Comfrey, Minnesota, was located in Brown County, the pheasant capital of the Midwest. With only 650 people in town, all roads leading to it from all four directions were bumper-to-bumper cars for at least five miles. The hunters were coming for their three pheasants, the legal limit of the day. I knew nothing about "pheasant under glass." I only knew we were going to eat well with the meat and gravy and all of the special sides during this season.

The sounds and smells remain etched in my memory. First the smells. Crisp fall leaves and foliage crunching under heavy boots. There was usually a chill in the air. A shot rang out here and there. Voices of businessmen from the city coming to the country and taking a break from their routine. Always the smell of cigarettes and the city folk who smoked cigars—rich-smelling, expensive cigars. You could actually smell their clothes as they arrived. They smelled new and heavy; they were made of nice wool and had beautiful colors. There was the smell of fall foliage, and often the smell of smoke as farmers burned the stalks and stubble left from harvested crops, and families in town burned leaves. Kitchens were busy roasting the catch: pheasants and an abundance of fall vegetables.

Excitement came to my little town for the three-week hunting season. My dad felt important because he knew where to take these "city folk" for the best hunting. I would often ride in the car with them as a scout for the prey. Once, they let me shoot a gun. I steadied it on my shoulder and pulled the trigger. The kick was huge and I was small. It threw me to the ground!

Everyone thought that was so cute. They laughed and I laughed too. I felt very included.

There was a university professor, a doctor, and a lawyer who regularly came to our house. They were friends of my uncle in the city and my dad was their annual tour guide. They brought gifts for my mom and us children. There were not too many opportunities in our little town to feel so important and I was proud of my dad for knowing where to take the hunters. For a short while, he was the one with the skills and knowledge. Pride swelled in my chest and my thoughts were that he was a "street-smart man."

LESSONS LEARNED

From the pheasant hunters I learned that some places must be very different from my home. They looked, dressed, and acted differently from the men in my farming community. They made me curious. They always were nice to me, but I wondered more about city men.

Smells and Memories

"All we have to believe is our senses, the tools we use
to perceive the world: our sight, our touch, our memory.
If they lie to us, then nothing can be trusted."

—Neil Gaiman

As though they were sealed in a vault, our sense of smell locks in memories that are reawakened with pungent smells. One of my childhood—maybe even preverbal—smell memories is the smell of nicotine and alcohol. It is at the same time familiar, comforting, awful, safe, and threatening, pulling me toward it and pushing me away.

Those smells meant that my mom and dad were near. It means that something bad was going to happen. It meant that I was in a territory with people that loved me and it meant there was no one there for me. I always knew that cigarettes and alcohol were more important than me, but I knew I was a close third. It was my smell of my childhood and my teen years. I also married a smoker the first time around. It was only with my divorce that I realized that I hated the smell and would never live in that environment again.

Perhaps the strongest feelings I associate with cigarettes and alcohol are anger, loss, confusion, and loneliness. Smells have also brought me great comfort, and those smells are also part of my memory bank.

Cinnamon rolls. Amy, a grand baker who worked for a bakery, was my mom's good friend. Many a day in my growing-up years, I would come home to smell them baking in the oven. Amy would bring a pan of them to our house and Mom would put them in the oven to be ready when I got home from school. I am not sure if it was the sweet, warm rolls alone I recall so fondly, or if it was having the company of my mom and Amy waiting to hear about our day after school that made it special.

Sunday dinner. It was a three-week rotation of beef roast, pork roast, or chicken every Sunday after church. The meal of meat, the onions, and the side dishes—each prepared perfectly—is something I still try to create from time to time. It meant we were together for a couple of hours.

Cold tuna and macaroni salad. Yes, there was an aroma to this salad made with great homemade mayonnaise. Each Sunday afternoon, I made a huge bowl and kept it in a cake pan in the refrigerator. In addition to the cinnamon rolls, I would have a bowl of macaroni. All this snacking at four o'clock in the afternoon didn't keep me from eating a full supper as well. Again, was it the companionship or the food? I don't know.

Powder and Blue Waltz perfume. My grandma was always busy baking doughnuts. We had our own doughnut shop as she made dozens for the local café and the bowling alley. I grew up on doughnuts. She also fried a great hamburger. Even with the smells of hamburger grease and doughnut spices part of her daily life, Grandma still had flair and wanted to be an attractive woman. Working long and late hours, there wasn't always time for a bath and she didn't have a shower.

Her way of dealing with everyday smells was to wear a little lilac face powder and a dab of Blue Waltz perfume. I loved both smells and can bring back the closeness I felt with my Grandma by taking in the fragrance of lilacs or by opening one last bottle of Blue Waltz that I keep in my crystal cabinet.

It seems like we all have memories that are kept in our emotional vault that can take us to people and events that we have loved or hated. Letting go of the hard memories becomes important as we try to recreate or give ourselves the opportunity to find the memories that heal our hearts and feed our souls. These are some of the things that trigger many memories for me. Can you think of your own?

★ Foods that trigger happy times
★ Perfumes and lotions that tell a story
★ Fresh-cut grass
★ Flowers; for me it's lilacs, carnations, and roses
★ Candles

* ★ Campfires and fireplaces
* ★ The air after a rainstorm
* ★ New car smell
* ★ Baby powder and babies in general
* ★ Pizza or Italian restaurants
* ★ Trees

LESSONS LEARNED

I learned to trust my senses. When I smelled baking in the kitchen, I knew something good was going to happen, and when I smelled my grandma's perfume, I felt a feeling of safety and love. On the other hand, smelling cigarettes and alcohol made feel afraid, lonely, and left out.

Special Aunts: My Family Sages

*"The qualities I most admire in women
are confidence and courage."*

—Oscar de la Renta

My childhood years were filled with wonderful women, and they taught me a great deal. One of the reasons there was so much time for me to spend with these women is because my mom worked a great deal with my dad. They were inseparable. I was the first grandchild in the family and loved by all. It was many years before there were more female grandchildren. It seemed I was everyone's daughter and the only female grandchild in my early years. I can remember getting stomachaches because of the tension that came with everyone wanting me to come stay with them and my difficulty having to make a choice.

Elaine was the aunt I watched, *really* watched. She was pretty and sweet and always had her beautiful red hair done well. She lived in the city and wore pretty clothes. Elaine was like a princess and she taught me how to dress and be "a girl." Later, when I moved to the city, her home became my home. Her polish and sophistication were not lost on me.

Lorrie moved into our house when she graduated from high school. She was ten years older than I. She married one of my dad's friends. She bore nine children, eight girls and a boy. She raised each child with love, values, decency, laughter, skills, and a love of God. To this day, each has become a gift to the families they have created and the communities they serve. She taught me through her loving and simple presence.

Gertie was on my dad's side of the family. His family was very splintered, but she took being my godmother very seriously. She cooked for me, told me family stories, and introduced me to something I had not experienced before—a white porcelain bathtub. It made me feel like a princess. She taught me to love my extended family.

Harriet was married to my uncle, who was also my godfather. She was a teacher and she was so smart. Harriet always talked to me about saving money for her children to go to college. She increased my restlessness in a good way, because she showed me it was good and important for women to be smart and educated.

LESSONS LEARNED

My aunts and Grandma were the first women in my life that served as mentors and teachers. They always made me feel special and that started very early in life.

What Is Being Poor?

"Wealth consists not in having great possessions,
but in having few wants."

—Epictetus

I didn't realize until I was grown up just how poor our family was during my childhood years.

Our garden was lush and had a little fence around it. In the summer, there were flowers everywhere and my mom's purple clematis was the talk of each summer. The bedroom I shared with my sister was pretty. My dad traded some of the wares from his business to farmers so our meat was fresh and free of preservatives, and our eggs were straight from the farm.

My clothes were mostly made from the colored and patterned feed sacks at my dad's hatchery. Because I got first choice of the feed sacks, it never occurred to me that we were poor and my clothes were being made out of feed sacks. I thought the poor people were the ones that had to go to the store to buy ready-made clothes, or the ones who got the "not so pretty" feed sacks after my first choice.

Granted, we had only one bathroom for seven people, but that was a step up from my grade-school years when we only had an outdoor bathroom and used Sears catalogues for toilet paper. Now we had toilet paper on a roll and didn't have to go outdoors in wintertime.

Another sign of my good fortune was the wonderful basket full of cold meat, cheese, and homemade doughnuts that my grandma would bring when I went on one of our frequent train rides together. I thought the poor people were the ones that had to go to the dining car because they didn't have a grandma who brought such good food.

My dad was a good cook as well. His specialities were homemade butter each Sunday morning, pickled pigs' feet, headcheese, liver and onions, and homemade horseradish. Strong and powerful tastes for a little girl, but I loved them all.

Our school band director lived on one side of us. Having him as a neighbor was a sign that we were part of the community. He was beloved by all in the town; having him living next door was a sign of status because it was such a contrast to our other neighbors. The Tomlins lived on the other side. The mom was young, about twenty years old. Her husband, in his mid-fifties, had "won" her in a poker game. Their house was messy and they were poor enough that people from the county brought them food every week. The dad did odd jobs and the girls were friends with my sister and me. Every week when they got their county food, it included a big block of cheese, and for a few days we all shared cheese and crackers. I thought maybe they were poor. I felt lucky to be rich.

Our food was fresh from the garden or canned by my mom and aunt. My mother was a terrific cook, as were my grandma and my aunts. We had a big garden and in the summer there were plenty of fresh vegetables; in winter we would open the jars they had preserved and canned. We always had good food. My dad often traded his services for a side of beef, and we had chickens at our hatchery. Even so, my mom, being thrifty, would carefully portion our food. There were always enough vegetables and bread. However, we could sometimes be a little short on meat and dessert.

Living in a small town, we would often have someone extra pop in when not expected. Someone Mom met at church, a neighbor, or someone one of us children would invite home before asking about it. When that would happen, Mom would choose one of us to say we didn't want any meat. Usually whoever did the inviting would decline meat, even when it was Mom. Then when it was time for dessert, she would simply say, "If you haven't eaten any meat, then you can't have dessert." That way, each guest could be accommodated.

LESSONS LEARNED

Being poor has to be clearly spelled out. I felt rich in my growing-up years, because the things that mattered were available: shelter, good food, generosity with sharing food, and clothes to wear. To this day, "enough" is always good enough for me. The feeling of richness is a feeling of safety and security and basic needs being met. Looking back, these values were always a part of my growing up. With grown-up eyes, it's easy now to see that we didn't have much money. However, life was rich.

Bathtubs

"Anyone who thinks heaven is not hot water
behind a locked door has forgotten
what it means to live."

—Lucy Frank

The first bathtub that I remember was a galvanized metal tub that my mom would bring in each Saturday and set up in our kitchen. We would have two big kettles on the stove that we filled with cistern water, rainwater collected and stored in our cistern. We would heat the two kettles of water for each person taking a Saturday night bath. The water was ultra soft and we added wonderful-smelling bath salts. It all felt so good. That was the Saturday night ritual. Never any real privacy, but everyone just minded their own bath and really didn't notice other people in the nearby rooms. In the winter, we had to pump water from a faucet in our kitchen.

In my high school years, we moved to a bigger house that had a bathroom with a metal shower in an indoor bathroom. Seven of us lived in that house: Mom, Dad, sister, brother, uncle, Grandpa, and me. We all took turns using the shower. It was quite perfunctory, and I missed the warm comfort of a hot tub. I longed for a bathtub.

There were, however, two homes I could go to that did have bathtubs. They were not galvanized, but white, comfortable, and inviting. One was at my Aunt Gertie's house. Her bathroom was as big as my bedroom and had cupboards, a chair, and a long mirror. I loved that room and took a bath every time I went to visit. The other was at the home of another aunt and uncle. The bathroom needed to be shared with other people, but it still was a major luxury and a safe place for me. Baths that were private, smelled very good, and were comfortable to touch became a sign of luxury for me.

There is a ritual to a bath. There must be bath oil and bubbles, and a big fluffy "feel-good" towel. I often like a cup of tea, a glass of iced tea, or a pretty glass of wine. In my recent homes, I also like to have a TV showing one of my favorite cooking shows or my specially selected Pandora music.

LESSONS LEARNED

Bathrooms with bathtubs are very important rooms in the house. They are a symbol for self-care and time alone. Often we all get too little of both. With spa music, candles, and relaxing fragrances, it can be a meditative and reflective time. On another night, maybe a good TV show and a glass of wine are the perfect relaxation. It can be whatever you choose on that day; it's just for you. On some really hectic days or days of stress, I have learned to take a warm to hot bath in the darkness with just one candle for light. No sound . . . it soothes me, helps me to unwind, and slows down all of the outside chatter.

Stockings: It's All About Status

"Healing comes from gathering wisdom from
past actions and then letting go of the
pain that the education cost you."

—Caroline Myss

Third grade was a time of big transition for me, but I didn't "get it" until years later. My parents moved from my birth town about one hundred miles away to a new town. My dad was going to have his own business and there was excitement in the air. We moved in the fall and school had already started. I was in the third grade.

The beginning of third grade was in a school where my grandma was the school cook. I had been going to school with her since I was about five years old in the first grade. I didn't turn six until November and was quite a bit younger than the rest of my class. By the third grade, I had friends and even a boyfriend. His name was Billy Joe Kickland. Everyone knew my grandma and she made sure I was safe.

Then came the announcement: we were moving 100 miles away. It was a scary time for me, but I needed to go along with the plans. When we arrived in our new town, Comfrey, Minnesota, there was another big change. I would now be going to a Catholic school. I had no experience with nuns and now I was going to be taught by them. They were scary to me, with their long black garments and white starched cloth around their faces. Two of them seemed kind; one was terrifying. Even the other nuns were afraid around Sister Lucy, the principal.

My mom bought my school uniform and long beige stockings that fastened with a clip under it. It all felt very strange to me. However, we moved in the fall of the third grade and I started Catholic school as soon as we arrived.

I was so busy and anxious with all the changes, and the fact that they didn't have a desk available for me, so I had to share a desk and a bench with another girl. I tried hard to be nice and to fit in. The girl I shared with was kind to me. I noticed the other girls watching me, but I didn't know why. Finally after a few days, I realized I was different. All the other girls had white, shiny long stockings. I was the only one with beige stockings made of rough cotton. When I finally noticed, I was surprised. To me, there was no meaning in the fact that my stockings were different. It was only as time went by that I realized that I had cheap, rough stockings and everyone else had pretty, smooth, white stockings.

I remember not wanting to have my mom find out about me being different. I knew she would feel bad because she would think she had made a mistake. I never did tell her and I don't think she ever knew. Eventually, as I moved up in grades, the difference in stockings became a thing of the past and I became part of the group. My embarrassment over my stockings faded.

LESSONS LEARNED

There were many ways I knew we were different, but I hadn't thought that much about them. Not having a bathtub and having different stockings all through Catholic grade school were just two of many differences. However, my family made me feel like I always had enough and in some ways I even felt rich. Perspective is such an interesting trait. As Henry David Thoreau said, "Things do not change; we change."

Abandoned

"When loneliness is a constant state of being,
it harkens to a childhood wherein neglect
and abandonment were the
landscape of life."

—Alexandra Katehakis

During my childhood, many hours were spent with Mom and Dad and their friends. They would be drinking, laughing, and oftentimes talking about things they didn't want me to hear. I was the only child in the group and often felt "left out." It was a type of rejection. I didn't feel I belonged to this group. That was when I first noticed the feeling of the "inside me" and the "outside me."

On the outside, I would act happy and be a good girl. On the inside, I was feeling hurt, angry, and alone. Many times I felt very dark and sad. Once, when I was five or six, my parents went out with friends. They left me alone sitting by myself in a nearby small town at a theater showing a movie about the singer Mario Lanza. I remember the movie starting and finishing, and then starting and finishing again. This happened several times before they realized they had forgotten me in the theater and returned to get me.

It seemed there were not many carefree times as a child. There also seemed to be someone that I was supposed to make happy. In some ways, it gave me great self-worth, but in other ways, it was very sad. I did believe there was a God and in my faith, I felt a connection.

There was always my prayer closet (to be explained later) and my grandma, who made me feel special. Basically, however, I was a loner. Many hours were spent playing games, cutting people out of the Sears and Roebuck catalogues, and creating happy families, children, and special events in paper dolls. Many hours also passed creating entire communities out of Lincoln Logs and Tinker Toys. I also loved to color and always had a coloring book nearby.

I created a mud bakery on my aunt's farm out in a grove. Even as an older child, I would make up large bowls and pans out of mud. I would then make cakes, pies, and cookies out of mud and decorate them with leaves, stones, and twigs. It brought me great joy to create, whether it was with Lincoln Logs, Tinker Toys, mud, rocks, or crayons.

LESSONS LEARNED

What I learned by being left in a movie theater alone is that I didn't come first. I knew that my parents were with Dorace and Glen and Bill and Mary. When they all got together, many hours would fly by and they would forget I was lying on the couch, waiting to go home from a bar, or sleeping on a strange bed. I wasn't frightened, but the hours crawled by and I didn't know what would happen. I knew they would come eventually.

Brass Bed

"It's not about an organized religion,
it's about developing a belief system
and part of that is faith."
—Sharon Wegscheider-Cruse

My faith started when I was very young. There used to be a type of headboard on brass beds that had little holes as a motif. There would be 100 or so little holes as the main decoration. Living in a little town, we also had a telephone office with telephone operators, much like the one that Lily Tomlin used to play as a character on *Laugh-In*. You would pick up these cords and insert them into the telephone board and make the connections for the people who were making the calls. Many days, I would stop at the telephone office and watch the operators work. Our little town had about four telephone operators.

Then this idea occurred to me. Maybe my headboard could be my board and pencils tied to the frame would just fit into the little holes. So I tied about ten pencils to my frame and there was my own connection headboard.

Growing up Catholic, after going to bed in the evening, I would think about all the things I wanted to pray to God about and would pick up a pencil and make the connection. Occasionally, I would pray to an angel and use another pencil. Of course, I knew most of the saints and had special saints for special circumstances. St. Anthony would help me find forgotten or lost items, St. Francis would help my garden and flowers grow, St. Joan of Arc would help me have courage, and St. Jude helped me with impossible situations. My brass bed connection with my God, as I believed, helped me through many tough situations.

LESSONS LEARNED

My brass bed was such a center of faith. What I learned by watching the telephone operators was a system of connection. Therefore, if I could find a way to connect with my God, I would stay safe. It filled many hours for me that could have been dark and empty. Instead, I was full of possibility.

Stuttering and Speaking:
Finding My Voice

"Don't carry your mistakes around with you.
Instead, place them under your feet and use them as stepping stones.
Never regret. If it's good, it's wonderful.
If it's bad, it's expensive."

—Alison Cross-Jones

As a young child, I often stuttered and talked very softly and had to be told to speak up. There was always activity in my home and it was often hard to get in the flow of conversation. Luckily for me, my Uncle Vern was a traveling salesman who came through my hometown about every month or two.

On one visit, he listened to me telling him a story and after I finished, he said, "Sharon, you are a smart little girl, but you will have to learn to talk better." I trusted him as he always showed such a loving interest in me. Then he said, "This is what we're going to do. When I come and visit, we will practice how to speak and then you will be given a subject. On my next trip, you have to have a little speech ready for me about that subject."

He would show me how to hold my head, how to make eye contact, when to smile, and when to pause. Then he would assign me a subject. Some I remember to this day are dogs, ketchup, tornadoes, churches, and colors. My speeches started out at two minutes and, after a few years, eventually I was speaking for forty-five minutes. As an adult, after twenty-five years of public speaking, I gave a keynote address for a national event. He sat in the front row. As I walked out of the green room to a music group bringing me onstage, from the podium I could see the tears glistening in his eyes. His favorite statement to me was, "Small-town girl makes good."

LESSONS LEARNED

What I learned from Uncle Vern is that I could better myself if I wanted to. It was possible and even fun. He made me feel important and able to speak up more when I needed to. I felt brave after he would come to visit.

Spirituality and Holy Hell as a Child

"Growing up happens when you start having things
you look back on and wish you could change."

—Clary Fray

My childhood was rich, poor, loving, and chaotic, and full of times of belonging—and times of isolation. There was drinking and drinking times that frightened me, but I didn't talk about it to anyone. Instead, prayer became my safe space and gave me solace.

My bedroom was on the second floor of our house and had a big closet on each side. My clothes were in one closet. In the other, I built a church. It was a good-sized closet. I lined up my dolls and teddy bears facing the front where I built a small altar. As a young child, whenever the Spirit moved me, I would go into the closet and preach to my heart's content about the world. I would talk about the sad, scary, and hopeful parts. Speaking and sharing my thoughts and feelings became an important part of my life. I had my dad put a lock on my church closet so my friends and family wouldn't look in there.

Holy Hell

When I was about nine years old it was already clear to me that spirituality and religion were two different things. To me, God was all the things that I learned from my aunts and my grandma. What I experienced with the nuns in Catholic school was something else.

The structure of the Catholic Church and many of its rules were frustrating for me. There had been many clashes in grade school between me and the principal, Sister Lucy. We butted heads all of the years I spent in that school.

Once I had to anonymously report her to the county for lack of cleanliness. After a spontaneous spot check by the county board of health, she was cited and sent to a training class. It was the right thing to do to protect us students, and it was empowering for me to see her have to respond and make changes.

There was a long history of my wanting to be an altar girl, but they only allowed boys to serve on the altar. The frustration grew when my desire to be a priest had no place to go. The idea of a female Catholic priest was considered absurd and disrespectful. I did, however, finish eight years of Catholic grade school.

Later in life, I found out that nuns were real people, with histories, lives, and their own back stories. When I was young, they seemed mysterious, powerful, controlling, and (once in a great while) nice to talk to.

Because Sister Lucy loomed so large in my life, I will start with her and then tell the story of the other nuns. Sister Lucy was *big*. I don't really know how big by height and weight, but her power was gigantic. She was the principal of the eight-grade school I attended. There were two other nuns teaching in the school, and because I went there for six of the eight grades, I experienced them all.

Sister Lucy was mean. When boys misbehaved, she gathered all the students to watch their punishment. She would have them lie over a desk and then she would hit them with a leather belt. To this day, I cannot bear to watch human violence, bullying, or cruelty, and I know that my fear started with this punishment routine. If you were a girl, you had to hold your hands out in front of you and she would hit them with a ruler. If it was winter, you had to hold your hands out the window until they were cold, and then she would hit them. It was like living under a cloud, not knowing when the storm would come. My stomach was always on alert.

Sister Beatrice was my third-grade teacher. She was small and very old. I knew she was in charge, but she was never cruel. I was not afraid of her. Sister Peona was my teacher as well as my piano teacher. I would go to the entry room of the nuns' convent where there was an upright piano; I took several years of lessons. I liked her and found her intriguing. Her skin was white and pink, and she was pretty with big brown eyes. Her voice had a softness to it and for a while she felt like a bigger, safe sister. If she would go over the time on a lesson, Sister Lucy would knock on the door and I would watch Sister Peona startle, with a look of fear in her eyes.

LESSONS LEARNED

By the time I was out of grade school, the idea of being a nun had lost its charm. I learned that wanting to become a nun was a stepping stone to what I really wanted: I wanted to become a priest.

Childhood Resiliency

"A good half of the art of living is resilience."
—Alain de Botton

Living in an alcoholic or any other dysfunctional family is never the easiest way to develop resilience, and yet it can be the surest way. Resiliency is a way of recovering quickly or "bouncing back" from difficulty or trauma. It is strength and courage that goes on.

There are many kinds of resilience. The first kind is emotional because it's our primary way of reacting. When our emotions have been triggered and we want to have knee-jerk reactions, resilience helps us slow down and feel the feelings, but curb the reaction. We can apply some reason and choice in the matter. We develop the ability to tolerate not knowing and uncertainty, and we can choose to respond appropriately or explode.

Physical resilience is also important. How we live determines how flexible and strong we become: the way we eat, the exercise we do or do not do, and how we care for ourselves by getting enough rest and sleep.

Decision-making resilience helps us make choices for ourselves that are good in the long run. We do not have to feed our every whim, appetite, or desire. We can take the time to think things through and make the best choices we can. We also don't have to fall victim to what happens to us. We can make choices on our own behalf.

Resiliency is one of the gifts we receive and can build on in times of crisis or loss. Parents who do everything for their children too often hamper the child's ability to build resiliency. It is through stress and strain that we each learn to make our personal peace with disadvantages and difficult times.

My resilience was strong and I was able to extract some special memories from difficult challenges that still fill my heart today.

LESSONS LEARNED

Even though as an adult today I recognize there were many problems in my family as a child, mostly I am able to take the learning and leave the rest. I know that I am resilient.

Chapter Two

HIGH SCHOOL YEARS

Growing Up

"Share our similarities, celebrate our differences."
—M. Scott Peck

Even though I went to public high school, there was still much involvement with the church. I learned to take the best it had to offer and leave the
rest. Church was an ongoing outlet for a great deal of creativity stored inside
me. Church could be both positive and negative, but the faith developed
through the church was affirming, empowering, and stabilizing in an otherwise often unstable time.

These years were spent in a small Minnesota Catholic church. Even though
there were dark secrets in the homes of many of the families, a lack of resources
that children needed, and way too much poverty, it was a typical village that
provided fun, laughter, music, and a sense of belonging. It was a fifties town
with a real diner, drugstore, liquor store, two grocery stores, a local newspaper,
movie theater, feed store, and even a clothing store.

I knew I had grown up when I was able, as a teenage girl, to walk into a women's clothing store and ask for feminine products. We didn't have a drug-store in my little town, only a pharmacy, so feminine products were sold at the clothing store. They were wrapped in brown paper so I could carry them home without feeling embarrassed.

Yet, there was a growing need and wish inside me that there was more going on in the world, but I couldn't find it and didn't know about it. It felt like the world was going by and somehow I was not a part of it. My soul was restless.

It was about this time that I started hearing arguments between my mom and dad late at night. I shared a room with my sister, and we would lie in bed and be frightened when they started arguing. My brother slept in a bed in my parents' room. I could imagine what it must have been like for him. Over time, the arguments worsened and were about even more things.

Somehow, even as a little girl and young woman, I knew that, "If it is to be, it is up to me." That was an *inside knowing*. Imagine my surprise as an adult to learn that that quote comes from William H. Johnsen, urging people to take responsibility for themselves. It's also an adopted theme song for all who grow up in painful, addictive, or dysfunctional families.

My mom was a very good housekeeper, but I wanted things really beautiful and nice as well. It was my job to fill a bug-spray bottle with good-smelling liquid from the Watkins Man (a door-to-door company that sold home prod-ucts) and spray it around the house after cleaning so the house would smell wonderful. Then, with the addition of freshly picked flowers, everything was nice. It made it possible to get away from the smell of cigarettes and alcohol. Now it was like my friends' houses.

My high school years widened the gap between my life outside my home and what was happening inside it. With coaching from my uncle, and a loving and talented speech teacher, my ability to speak and debate blossomed into local, regional, and state awards. My name was in newspapers, and it made my family proud.

LESSONS LEARNED

I learned that high school was very different from Catholic grade school. It was new and the other teens were different. I seemed to have more confidence. Being in a small-town high school was fun and I was growing up. However, when I went home after school, I wondered about what was going to happen. I became afraid when my parents argued.

Two Alcoholic Parents

"However long the night, the dawn will break."
—African Proverb

Most of my high school days were spent in a home where drinking played a major role almost every day. My father was one of my favorite people in the world. He died of alcoholism when he was forty-six. It said suicide on his death certificate, but alcoholism was the root cause. He loved me and was proud of me. He worked hard to give me the best he had.

My mother was chemically dependent on both alcohol and prescription pills. Both my parents were smokers. However, Mom did her best as well to give me a good home. She always had her little tin box where she saved coins so I would have money for extras, such as a class ring, high school photos, a pretty prom dress, and other things. Looking back with grown-up eyes, I do believe they gave me all they had, and much more than they ever had been given.

They both had two personalities. One personality was present when they were not drinking, and the other came out once drinking started. I tried to make sense of it and figure out what I could do to help them. It felt like "crazy making." Why would someone drink when they knew it was going to start trouble? Eventually, I realized that I couldn't stop the drinking. So I learned what to do once it started. I became clever, resilient, creative, and hypervigilant so I could protect myself. Life was often an emotional roller coaster.

The suffering that goes on is like a form of post-traumatic stress disorder (PTSD). This trauma goes well into adulthood for children who live in alcoholic homes. This impact needs healing. With knowledge, awareness, emotional release, and behavior change, there is hope. Eventually the "crazy making" can stop—but I am way ahead of my story.

LESSONS LEARNED

What I was learning as a youth was that my home life and my school life were very different in terms of the people and the feelings. I felt safer in school than at home sometimes. It felt a bit crazy.

Inside Life and Outside Life

"One thing I have learned to ask myself:
what is this situation trying to teach me?"
—Sharon Wegscheider-Cruse

As you might guess, I was very involved at school. I was president of several clubs, was homecoming royalty, had roles in class plays, competed in drama events, and wrote for the school newspaper.

My social life was full of friends, with three best friends and lots of slumber parties. I dated two boys. One was local, and the other was older and from the town that had the dance hall. Every Thursday night was the same during those years. First, there would be a visit to church for the service at Our Mother of Perpetual Help, and then into the car to drive fifteen miles to a neighboring town and dance out my heart and soul with a live orchestra. It was a quite a night for me.

At home, my dad's drinking was getting much worse. His business, however, was prospering, and it seemed that he and Mom were having fewer arguments. My mom actually joined him in the business and began to develop a role for herself. My sister and brother were both in grade school.

I started writing small little booklets and discovered that writing was something that filled my soul and, for a short time, gave some sense of order and peace to my life.

In a movie (*Family Reconstruction*) that I made with Virginia Satir, the family therapist and author, I referred to my late grade school and early high school years as my family's "golden" years. My father added new businesses and we finally had a small version of what today would be called a strip mall. He sold Norge appliances as well as radios, Zenith TVs, record players, and more. The hatchery was producing hundreds of baby chicks each Monday morning, and there was a gas station, a feed store, and bottled gas sales for the whole community. My dad worked hard, drank hard, and lived hard. Yet he was a loving, sweet man when not intoxicated. Each spring he filled his front window with colored baby chicks and gave them away to children. He hand-dipped every chick in Easter-colors dyes.

LESSONS LEARNED

I learned that "crazy making" was somewhat normal and to be expected. Another lesson was to find activities that could bring me some comfort. Writing was one of those. Lastly, I knew I loved my dad and that he was a sensitive man. It was hard to know my mother. She was always busy. However, I knew she was a good woman.

Alcohol and Cigarettes

"Be kind—for everyone is fighting a hard battle."
—Plato

As a young child, I realized there didn't *seem* to be a *problem* with alcohol in my home. It usually meant laughter, company coming over, a picnic, a holiday, or some gathering of family and friends. It was clear that any event that would take place would include alcohol.

I was puzzled, however, by my Aunt Harriet and Uncle Cecil. At my house there were all kinds of liquor: eggnog (with brandy at Christmas); gin and tonic for summer nights; beer for ball games; Bloody Marys for Sunday morning; and flavored gin (lemon, orange, and lime) mixed with soda to teach the children how to drink. I knew which alcohol went with each event by the time I was in early grade school.

But when we went to Harriet and Cecil's house, they had only one bottle of liquor (kept in their clothes closet) that they brought out on holidays to give all the adults one highball each to celebrate. My parents found that funny.

The other thing evident as a child was that my aunts and uncles did not smoke cigarettes. Once in a great while, an aunt would have one cigarette. My parents, however, had cigarettes all day and all evening. We lived differently. I didn't make judgments, but I hated the smell of both alcohol and cigarettes. Most of the time, our house smelled of really good food cooking, alcohol, cigarette smoke, and full ashtrays.

Everyone laughed when my dad would drive home *in* the ditch so as not to have a car accident while drinking. He often passed out and slept on the floor. I would lift his head and put a pillow under his head and lay a blanket over him. Often I would tuck my teddy bear in his arms. We lived one mile from my grade school. Early in the morning, my dad would go to his work, have a couple of drinks, and then come home to drive me to school. I could smell the alcohol.

Over time, there was more arguing between my mom and dad. There was less money and no more vacations. No one talked about the stress and changes, but I knew something was very wrong. When I got married at twenty, I remember telling my parents that I wanted to leave right after the toasts at my wedding reception. I knew that once alcohol was served, the atmosphere would change—and, bride or not, I didn't want to be there.

Interestingly enough, as far as I know, no one in my high school class ever had a drink in high school and no one smoked a cigarette. When I went back for my twenty-fifth high school reunion, there was no one who drank excessively and no one who smoked cigarettes.

I was an adult before I let my consciousness acknowledge that my family was very troubled by alcohol and also the addictions of smoking and gambling. Sir Walter Scott said it best: "Oh what a tangled web we weave/when first we practice to deceive."The most serious deception is the one we practice on ourselves.

LESSONS LEARNED

From a very early age, I knew alcohol and cigarettes were the most important things in the world in my family's house. After that came family, children, ideas, plans, work, etc. I learned to hate the smell of alcohol and cigarettes, and developed a knot in my stomach when I knew trouble was coming.

Mrs. Mett, My Speech Sage

"Why fit in when you were born to stand out?"

—Dr. Seuss

Following my Uncle Vern's tutoring, which is where I learned to love speaking in public, I met my high-school speech teacher. She was a young wife and mother and nurtured me in special ways. She used to stay after class and talk to me about writing and speaking. I loved listening to her dreams and all that she felt about learning and influencing the world. It was only when she was ninety and wrote to me that I found out that ours had been the first class she had taught.

It was not until then that I realized the importance of what had gone on in my small-town high school with her as our speech teacher. She told me that we had changed our high school in general and me in particular. As someone who had been painfully shy when I met her, I realized later that she had brought out the best in me. At the same time, she confessed that my work helped her feel and demonstrate her skills as a teacher.

Together, we put our little town on the map with our awards and winnings in original oratory and speech as we competed all over the state. With a microphone, today I feel confident and excited. This device has taken me around the world: into board rooms, national conferences, radio stations, and TV studios. I love the audience response, the meeting of eyes, and the connection that can be made between speaker and audience.

Mrs. Mett did not seek fame or glory. She did her best in the circumstances she was in. She was happy to watch others get the spotlight, while she fed her soul by knowing she was an amazing teacher. I was lucky to have known her and be a recipient of all she had to offer. My gratitude is profound. The following is an excerpt from a letter from Mrs. Mett:

Dear Sharon,

At 90, I live in an independent living complex in Minnesota. I have always loved your class. You were my first attempt at speech and you took me to the state finals three years in a row. I learned more on the job than I taught. Your bright class was so good that I really STUDIED in order to teach you. I will never forget YOU and your energy and talent at original composition, which you delivered with equal zest. I know we wowed the whole district by our main entries and good marks, and then to the state.

You turned out to be interest on an investment. I am in bliss and call you a disciple simply because you took up the disciplines I taught. You transported me. I am grateful that God brought you into my life. I had wanted to be a missionary, and after all is said and done I think I was. I was able to give troublesome teens guidance and they themselves had good careers. Mr. Klomps (the principal) said your class turned out to be really good citizens and he was proud as well.

You have rewarded me and set the world on fire. You bring me Joy. I love you.

Mrs. Margaret Mett

LESSONS LEARNED

From Mrs. Mett, I learned that I was a different person away from home. She was always so happy to see me and she had such faith in me. From her, I learned to try hard, to laugh, to create, and to feel good about myself. I felt like we were a winning team, and I felt safe with her.

Mr. Halos, My Business Sage

"My father was very generous and
a gambler by instinct, and died broke. The lesson he
wanted to teach me was not to worry.
The lesson I learned was to worry."

—Barbara Walters

By the time I reached high school, I knew we had less money than many of my friends, and money felt like safety. I cannot tell for sure how I knew, since my dad always had a wad of bills he carried in his pocket and that he would whip out when he chose.

There had been too much listening in the dark when my parents would talk and argue about money. My mom couldn't get the stainless sinks she so wanted for the kitchen; they were too expensive. There were jokes about an aunt and uncle and how much money they seemed to have. There were things we couldn't buy because they were too expensive. No one talked directly about what we did and did not have. But there was this vague, mysterious concern.

When I had the chance to take a business course with Mr. Halos, it was like there was something special there for me to learn. Taking that class was a walk on a different planet. Money was out in the open, and the earning, spending, and the saving of it was spoken about directly. My two years of business in that class have stayed with me all my life. It all made such good sense. Two financial fundamentals learned from Mr. Halos that have been incorporated into my life are:

1) Do not get caught up in the game of plastic. He called it "the easy payment plan." For many years, I kept jars with titles on them like clothes, entertainment, taxes, car, etc. I rationed out how much

could go in each jar, and when it was gone, there was no more. The jars were arranged in order of priority. It was only as an adult when having a credit card became absolutely necessary that my first card was issued. To this day, I have two credit cards and no credit card debt, ever. I refuse to pay interest because that money could be used elsewhere.

2) The second lesson learned was to save, save, and save some more. Ever since I took his class, saving has been a habit with me. He taught me that the goal of making money was to first take care of yourself and then save enough that your money would make money. Great goal, and I have worked toward that end since I was fifteen.

Whether I have been writing, speaking, counseling, consulting, or managing a corporation, I still use the business skills that started in high school with Mr. Halos.

LESSONS LEARNED

From Mr. Halos I learned that money was very important to help you find your safety and fund your dreams. He convinced me that it had to start in your early life and be followed all the way. He inspired in me the desire to manage my life by taking charge of what I could take charge of. Money was one thing that I could learn to manage, and that helped keep me from feeling powerless.

Hard Times

"No one escapes. Somewhere between birth and death,
we all run up against something we can
do absolutely nothing about."
—Jeanne Griffin

The "crazy making" times started in late grade school and became more frequent during high school. How could my family be so wonderful sometimes, and so angry and scary other times? At first, I thought something was wrong with me. Everybody loved coming to my home. My friends loved coming, and the extended family came very often. Our home was the center of action.

My small group of four special friends had many slumber parties at our house. They liked my parents and my parents welcomed everyone into our home. My very best friend Barbara and I slept in each other's homes about four days a week. I always felt popular and at school I was a part of everything. Class plays, writing for the newsletter, going to dances, flirting with the boys, attending church events—my high school life was rich.

Yet at home with my parents there were arguments and discord. My dad would slam doors and mother would cry. There was not enough money. I think the worst was the feeling of dread and heaviness and the expectation that something bad was going to happen.

Just enough bad things did happen to keep the fear of what could happen alive. Then we would have many good days. Maybe a trip to the lake, Grandma coming to visit, going fishing with my dad, and having a picnic at a softball game. We all learned to pretend that everything was okay.

Whenever the crazy feeling came, it was never that anything was wrong with my parents. It made me doubt myself and what was wrong with me.

Many times if I cried or seemed sad, the comment would be, "You are too sensitive," or "Get that long face back into a smile, you are making too much of something." Rarely, if at all, did I ever hear, "What are you feeling?" or, "What's wrong?" All feelings that were painful were ignored and my thoughts always went to "there must be something wrong with me."

LESSONS LEARNED

I learned that the only way I could survive all that was happening at home was to stay busy at school. The feeling of chaos and confusion was growing stronger each day. The only lesson I learned at that time was to try and build my own life and stay busy.

Sex Ed

"It is not sex that gives the pleasure,
but the lover."
—Marge Piercy

The little green book and a skeleton key were a big part of my sexual education. No one in my family ever offered me "the talk." However, in a little dresser in my parents' bedroom, there was a book that spelled out all the details of anatomy and what happens to make a baby. It's also the same little dresser where my dad kept all his photos from when he served in World War II. As I overheard family conversations, I realized that both subjects were off limits. If I asked my dad about his war years, his eyes would cloud over with tears and he didn't say much. Finally I quit asking, but I knew where the photos were and I went and looked at them. He scrap-booked and I still have his war photos.

While going through his photos, I found the little green book and began to read and look at the pictures. I learned many things I did not know. Somehow, I felt it was better not to ask questions of either of my parents about that subject and yet, I had many questions. At a "girl" party, I asked my twelve-year-old girlfriends what they knew about sex and mentioned what I had read in the little green book. One of the girls said it was all true, and if I wanted to know how it all worked, I could come and stay at her house on Saturday night—so I did.

We went to bed in her bedroom, but did not go to sleep. About midnight, we could hear her parents come into their bedroom, right next door. There was a door between her bedroom and their bedroom. It had a lock that worked with a skeleton key. This kind of lock was pretty big. She started watching through the keyhole and at a certain point, she invited me to look as well.

Her parents seemed happy; they were following the instructions that were given in the little green book and I got my education. Afterwards, I thanked my friend for my lesson and we both took the situation very seriously. It might have been nice to have this conversation with my mom, but a book and keyhole got the job done.

LESSONS LEARNED

What I learned about sex from watching my friends' parents was a loving learning. It made me feel good, and they seemed to really like being with each other. I hoped that someday I would feel that safe with someone. Having sex was good.

Social Life

"There are some days when I think I'm going to die
from an overdose of satisfaction."

—Salvador Dali

My high school days were filled with friends and activities. My grades were good and learning was of high value to me; it was opening doors to the world for me. Many of the skills I acquired—public speaking, typing, and business acumen—are important to me today. I was either an officer or a member of every club. The clarinet was my band instrument, and debating and oratory were activities in which I excelled. I was in both my junior and senior class plays and competed in one act dramas. Working on the newsletter all four years kept me busy after school hours.

There was the usual high school girls' clique and I was in it. Four girls became my special friends and even traveled with me to visit my extended family. My home was open to my friends; they really liked my house with the piano and we always had good food. Our home had the first television in town. My little town did not yet have cable; no picture, only what we called "snow." However, for two years my friends came to my house to "listen" to the television until a stronger signal came in. We had many parties with popcorn while we listened to Liberace and Milton Berle. It was so exciting two years later to get to see what they actually looked like!

In high school, I began to learn that there is more to life than the home life I had lead, and that I didn't have to be powerless. I could take action and produce the results I wanted. Another important learning was that there was so much more to learn—and I would have to leave home to learn it. The proms, dates, concerts, and parties taught me that I was liked, respected, and that more good things were to happen.

Each Sunday morning my uncle loaned me his car and I drove to Minneapolis 100 miles away to see the Minneapolis Lakers play basketball. I always stayed in a hotel or with my aunt. I also went to the Minnesota state basketball tournaments. At the tender age of sixteen, I could find the downtown hotels, rent a hotel room, and get around downtown. I always had a friend with me, but I felt so grown up.

LESSONS LEARNED

Many lessons were taught to me by my social life in high school. People liked me and I was popular. My grades were good and I felt smart. My girlfriends were close friends and I had a few special friends who would stay overnight with me or invite me to their homes. Some traveled out of town to my grandma's house with me, and some went to Minneapolis with me. I learned that there was more to life than what was happening in my home and that someday I could have my own home that would be as much fun as my friends' homes.

The Fire

"Weeping is not the same thing as crying.
It takes your whole body to weep and when it's over,
you feel like you don't have any bones left to hold you up."

—Sarah Ockler

On January 26, 1952 my family's lives changed forever. The little mall my father had built burned to the ground. This mall served the needs of the community. My father had put everything he could muster together into the building of the mall—but he skimped on insurance. People in small towns weren't as savvy about insurance as they are today.

There had been two previous big fires in Comfrey. Both buildings had been vital parts of the community. One was St. Paul's Catholic Church, the other was the primary grain elevator. In 1952, it was the Roelandt Hatchery. All three businesses were the core buildings in this little town. My parents were at a get-together with other business people, and I was babysitting at home just a block from the hatchery. It was 9:30 at night. I heard the fire trucks before I saw the fire. It was -26 degrees F. and all the fire hydrants were frozen.

My memory of that night is seeing firemen going in and out of our home, changing clothes in my parents' bedroom as their current clothes became frozen to their bodies. New clothes were brought in. Women and young people were in the kitchen making coffee and food. It felt like this whirlwind and terror went on for hours. Before the flames settled down into the snow, the whole building and shopping center was gone. Our life, as we knew it, was gone. I wept.

I was a freshman in high school and that night, as my mom and I walked out and looked at the ruins, she said, "You know, Sharon, you will never be able to go to college." I internalized that message and knew she was right.

I graduated from high school at seventeen in 1956. At the time, I had two boyfriends. They knew about each other. One was a local classmate, and the other lived in a bigger town nearby. Yet, at seventeen, I was not ready to marry—though some of my classmates did marry. I was restless, and since there was no money, I went to the biggest nearby city, Minneapolis, and went to work.

My dear aunt and uncle, the ones who had taught me to speak and helped me capture three state titles in debate and public speaking, invited me into their home in the city. Five days after high school graduation, I packed up and took the few things I owned and drove the 100 miles. I never went home to live again; I was on my own in every way, including financially.

Leaving home was very hard and traumatic for two different reasons. One reason is that my "inside self" knew the pain of my family. It had been two years since the fire, but my dad never recovered. My brother, sister, and mother needed so much. The years were so hard for my dad.

He was never able to find success again. Without insurance, he lost everything. All of his battles were always uphill. He began taking loans against our paid-for house. (We found that out later when we went to his safety deposit box after his death.) My mother, brother, and sister were penniless and relied on relatives to help them at that time.

The second reason it was hard to leave is that I was seventeen, had never experienced anything but small-town living, and I was afraid. Yet I knew I must go. When I left, I left home forever.

LESSONS LEARNED

What I learned with the fire was that my family lost everything; I could not go to college. I learned that my dad's life was over. I learned that it was not our fault; it just happened to us. I learned that life was going to be hard and that things would never be the same.

Chapter Three

BECOMING
RESPONSIBLE

Move to the Big City

"Follow your dreams.
Courage is the power to let go of the familiar."
—Raymond Lindquist

At seventeen, moving to a city was quite an experience. Living with people who loved me made it easier. However, all of the details were overwhelming. Learning how to take care of my car without my dad, paying for all my own clothes, and finding a doctor and a dentist were things I had never done before.

At seventeen, my inside self and outside self were widening. By this, I mean that all my feelings and emotions were becoming more painful and burrowing deeper inside, while, paradoxically, the part of myself that I showed to the world was of someone with no problems: looking and appearing better and better.

I was out of the home trauma, but my family was still in the throes of it. I felt guilt and hopelessness about their situation. There was also a glimmer of hope for me, but that only increased the guilt.

My salary as a secretary was $230 per month, but the job had health insurance and that was a help. My salary had to cover rent, auto expenses, food, clothes, and personal items. I also sent money home to help my brother and sister.

I had no training, but my high school typing and shorthand skills were excellent. Organization came naturally to me. With my experience as a speaker and writer, it seemed to my boss and office workers that I was more skilled and mature than I really was.

There was a music school in Minneapolis called MacPhail, where I volunteered in exchange for singing lessons. Later I learned to play the guitar and took great pride in singing in the church during the transition from organ hymns to guitar singing.

There was also an organization called Big Sisters. In my spare time, I volunteered to spend time with a ten-year-old girl. Her name was Henrietta and she was Native American. We spent many Saturdays together for a few years. I drove across the city to dance once a week at the Prom Ballroom. Looking back, I have compassion for the girl I was. I tried so hard to have a good life and, in many ways, I did.

On cold Minnesota nights, playing cards by the fire was a common pastime. My aunt and uncle taught me to play cribbage, and that was the beginning of my love for the game. We worked out an arrangement that turned on winning at cribbage.

Their car was in the garage, but mine was exposed to snow, ice, and rain. If I won at cribbage for the evening, my uncle would drive and pay for takeout from our favorite deli about four miles from the house. If I lost, he would still pay, but I had to go out on a bad weather night and pick up the food. That arrangement made me a very serious cribbage player. Ironically, my aunt was the best player and she always cleaned up after we ate.

LESSONS LEARNED

At seventeen, it was a shock to realize how much I took for granted in high school. Having to pay to live somewhere was a new experience, and paying for food was another shock. Paying for hoses and oil for my car was something I had done since I was sixteen, when I bought my first black Studebaker, which had pink terry cloth seats and wooden blinds in the windows.

Getting a job was exciting. My typing, shorthand, and speaking skills won me that first job as a secretary in a large organization. I felt sad not to go off to college like many of my friends. Yet, ever since the fire, there had been no way and no money. Working was my only hope at that time. It felt good to be hired by grown-up men who seemed to know what they were doing. It built my confidence to get a job within two weeks of interviewing.

Because of all my high school involvement, joining Big Sisters and taking music lessons seemed like an extension of my extracurricular work in high school.

Another important lesson learned was that one could live from day to day without cigarettes and alcohol use all the time. I liked that feeling of cleanliness.

Fairy-Tale Wedding

*"All changes, even the most longed for,
have their melancholy. For what we leave behind us
is a part of ourselves. We must die to one life
before we can enter another."*

—Anatole France

After about a year on the job, my boss asked me out for a date. He was twelve years older than I was, but we talked and worked well together. However, it was against company policy for employees and employers to date, so he asked if I would consider getting a different job. It would never have occurred to me to ask him to consider changing his job. So I went job hunting and found one right away with a competitor. It was the same kind of job in personnel, now human resources, and I moved across the street and proceeded to date my former boss.

We dated, but the split inside me was getting more intense. As life was getting better for me, it was getting harder for my family back home. I felt guilty about every good thing that happened to me. My trips home became less frequent. Seeing what was going on was too painful. Addiction was taking over my former home. My heart went out to my younger sister and brother, yet, I felt powerless. There was no way to help and no way not to hurt right along with them.

Meanwhile, my own life was manageable and getting better all the time. Tom and I planned our wedding. Twelve years my senior, he was ready to settle into the life he wanted, and we married.

I was nineteen. I had been on my own for two years, becoming whom I was to become: totally independent.

When my engagement led to the wedding six months later, I was living in two worlds. The town where I had lived until age seventeen had 550 people and 250 of them—nearly half the population— were invited to my wedding. Add my city friends and the number of people at our wedding swelled to 400. It was an enchanting service.

I wore twenty-two yards of satin, made into a gown that fit my ninety-nine pounds. The church and the grounds were full of people. The choir sang all my favorite songs, and my five bridesmaids were stunning. There was a ceremony where I made an oath to the Blessed Virgin Mother to be an honoring wife and mother, should I have children. Extended family and friends had come from all over the country. My heart was full of hope and commitment.

I had already made the decision not to be at my reception. We attended just long enough for a toast to be made and for us to greet our guests from the head table. Then, on a pretense of going to the restroom, we slipped out the back door and left on a two-week trip. This was to prevent seeing what I was sure was inevitable: the liquor and drinks would begin to flow and things would get angry and ugly. Not wanting my wedding memories to be ruined, I simply did not attend the reception. From all accounts afterward, my worst fears were realized.

LESSONS LEARNED

The biggest lesson here was to follow my gut. I knew enough people loved me and would come near and far to see me married. I knew I could be a princess in a princess wedding and that it would be a day to remember.

My knowing also told me it would end with a great deal of drinking and I would be embarrassed if I were to stay and watch it all unfold. Every special night that I could remember had ended that way.

Therefore, choosing to leave when the reception started was a wise decision. I learned early in life to be hypervigilant and to protect myself when a situation looked like it might go bad. This has saved me from many painful situations.

Eden Prairie:
My Own Home and Family

"The mind, once expanded to
the dimensions of larger ideas, never
returns to its original size."
—Oliver Wendell Holmes

Tom and I built a new home, a beautiful suburban house on several acres with forty full-grown trees. Everything was new, right down to the canary-yellow kitchen appliances. It was a true fifties home, and I became the fifties suburban wife. We made many friends and on the outside it looked like my life was to be envied.

Yet on the inside, chaos and fear were one phone call away. I can remember just wanting to sleep some days so as to not face the stress of living two lives. Over time, Tom began to resent the intrusion of my family and how their situation upset me.

The best thing that happened is that I became pregnant and was so happy I thought I would burst. Pregnancy was hard for me, and my doctor said it was due to my stressful lifestyle. Yet there had never been such happiness in my heart. My firstborn was a son and he has provided me with a lifetime of joy. His birth and infancy took up time that was formerly spent in worry, and so as soon as I could, I became pregnant again. Becoming a mother was the most awesome thing that ever happened to me.

My firstborn daughter was born two years later and this was the truest, cleanest pure love I had ever felt. This quote from Elizabeth Stone best expressed how I felt: "Making a decision to have a child—it is momentous. It is to decide forever to have your heart go walking around outside your body."

My children gave me the greatest joy I had ever felt, and raising them was becoming my first passion. Tom and I began to grow apart, but I tried to find ways to connect. He wanted all my time, and yet my family of origin was always in some kind of crisis. My worry for my younger sister and brother was there, my best friend who lived across the street and was my confidante was dying of cancer, and there was the daily care of my children, a toddler and a new baby. He resented all the time he didn't get from me.

We began to grow apart. He became self-absorbed with watching TV, reading, and doing things he could do alone. He treated me as though I was a nice addition to his life, but not a partner; I was more like an asset.

My husband's addiction to reading, financial news, and TV began to be a real issue as the children grew; I felt more and more like a single parent. There was no one with whom to share school stories, daily happenings, or concerns. We definitely were not having any fun as a family and I was desperately lonely. My children were so good and so very much fun. My sadness was growing.

At the same time addiction was growing in my family at home. One night, I packed up my children and went home to visit. My dad was out the night I arrived and came home very drunk. I had just begun to find my voice and I confronted him about his drinking. I told him how concerned I was for my sister and brother. He attacked me verbally and I could not believe it. He had always adored and respected me. The shock sent me to the phone the minute he passed out. At about midnight I found someone to drive me 100 miles home to Eden Prairie; I never went home again until the day my dad died.

Meanwhile, my mom's life began to unravel. Her brother feared she was dying and even the local physician gave up trying to help her. I found care for my children, and her brother and I drove her to the Mayo Clinic in Rochester, Minnesota. They saved her life. She had no insurance and they took her in as a charity case, for which I will always be grateful. That was the end of my past home life as I knew it.

LESSONS LEARNED

There were many lessons learned at my new home in Eden Prairie. I had acquired status as a young wife of a respected professional. My neighbors recognized me as sophisticated and smart. My children were born, and they were the biggest lesson of all. I found out that my capacity to love and protect was huge and I had given birth to babies that would become people I knew I would love for the rest of my life.

In the background was my family-of-origin trauma, but they took a backseat now that there was something precious of my own that demanded my attention. There was a joy that was new. I loved the hope of this time of my life.

I learned that my life was my own and I could create happiness and not only be a daughter of trauma.

My Dad's Suicide

"People do not die of suicide. They die from sadness."
—Anonymous

It was Christmas Eve. My baby girl was three months old and my son was two years old. My parents were coming to spend Christmas with us. I talked to my family that afternoon and they assured me they would be there in time for dinner.

We waited . . . and waited. I called home and the line was consistently busy. *Strange. They should be on their way.* Finally the phone rang and my dad's brother picked it up. He said, "Sharon, come home. Your dad is dead. We need you." Leaving my children with my husband's parents, we began the 100-mile ride, my mind racing all the way there. *Heart attack, car accident, stroke? What happened?*

As we pulled up in front of my old home, I saw the Christmas tree laying in the snow in the front yard. All the old familiar ornaments were laying in the snow. What happened? There were lots of cars around and through the window I could see lots of people. Why weren't they home? It was Christmas Eve. As I walked through the front door, I saw the local physician giving my mother a shot. She looked shocked and sleepy at the same time.

My uncle took me upstairs immediately. My sister and brother were huddled together in one of the bedrooms. He said, "Sharon, your dad committed suicide this afternoon." My dad was only forty-six years old.

I shut down. There was no taking in emotionally all of what was happening. There was much to do. My sister stayed with a local family while my mother, brother, and I began to make all the plans. Going to the bank, we found that the house was going to be repossessed upon my dad's death for loans taken out that we had not known about. We asked the bank for some time, which they granted, so we could handle all of the details of my dad's death, and then deal with the current problems we were facing financially. The funeral was as big as my wedding had been and it was so cold. It was New Year's weekend. We drove his body 100 miles to a Catholic cemetery in his hometown with a caravan of cars. In later years, we found out his grave is on the site of his home where he grew up until he was orphaned. He has truly gone home.

My mother stayed with relatives; my husband went back to Minneapolis to work the next day. I drove back to Comfrey, my hometown, to close up the house. Going back into that house was a mess. The Christmas tree was still in the yard, ashtrays were full, empty drink glasses were everywhere, food was on the counter, and it was cold. I spent the night cleaning up the house, dragging the tree to the backyard, washing dishes (there were no dishwashers back then), and putting everything in order. This was the home I had remembered. It was a pretty home and a comfortable one. I went to lock up the house before I remembered that we never had a lock on the house. We would go on trips and always just leave it open. This was a very safe little town.

Driving back to Eden Prairie, I began to thaw out a bit. Tears gently fell as my feelings started to come to the surface. There was such a deep longing for my own home and my children. Deep inside, there was a commitment to make my marriage work and not let this sadness ruin my marriage.

My husband was very angry that I was so involved in caring for my family of origin. Our distance widened. It was to a point of exhaustion. My two children and I became a unit, and he became a separate unit.

I truly believed in the goodness of God, a Higher Power, the Universal Energy, etc. My belief assured me that life was unfolding as it should, and I wanted very much to have a third child. It was important to me, and so our third child was born. She was a true Irish lass, with black hair and blue eyes, and was a treasure for our family. The older two hovered over her and thought she was a delight. She looked a lot like me when I was born, and she was a delightful child.

My mom and grandma were there for my children. However, my dad's drinking and behavior had distracted my mom. Oftentimes, I felt alone and insecure about the safety and well-being of my children—I wanted so much more for them.

LESSONS LEARNED

I learned that no matter how hard we try, there are things beyond our control. I tried to be a good person, a good daughter, and a good family member. My dad chose to die. For many years, I did not accept that that is what he chose to do. Virginia Satir (that story is coming) took me to the place of giving that decision back to my dad.

My home was forever different and would never be there again for me. I learned that life is fragile.

I learned not to count on anyone to be there for me. I learned to numb the depth of my feelings. I learned that my family of origin was affecting my marriage. I learned that I felt very alone. I learned that I loved my dad, but he could never hear me again. I froze emotionally.

Prayer Table

"The life of the Spirit is not for the weak-hearted.
It means venturing into unknown territory."
—Sharon Wegscheider-Cruse

I felt like a single parent. My children were great, yet I was desperately lonely. We weren't fun as a family or as a couple.

This was such painful time. I went to counselors by myself because my husband refused to go. I read books, I wrote him ten-page letters when he wouldn't talk to me. I so wanted to save this marriage. We went to a marriage encounter program and were the only couple that didn't graduate; Tom refused to engage in the program. Some days were full of anguish.

The only break in the pain was belonging to a church where I had many friends. The priest there asked Tom and me to join a group of six married couples who wanted to improve their relationships. It was shocking to have Tom say he would go. It was called an encounter group and was actually a PhD project for the local priest, who was becoming a psychologist. We met every week and one full weekend a month for two years. Every other couple in the group flourished and loved the program, but not us. It was clear our relationship was not going to work.

Following this program, I asked Tom for a divorce. He said no, and if I divorced him, he would not support the children or me. My family of origin was in its own crisis and so I stayed. I had nowhere else to go. We moved to a new house, hoping it would help.

While in the encounter group, I bonded with the other people and they are friends still today. For the first time, I realized that *I* was not the problem. Tom's refusal to connect with anyone, including me, was a big part of the problem. My confidence grew just a bit. We struggled on.

LESSONS LEARNED

This group was a great teacher for me. The most important lesson was that my ideas and perceptions were very similar to everyone else's in the group and also to the facilitator's. For so long, it had felt to me that I was out of sync with the rest of the world. Certainly, my thoughts, feelings, and behaviors had been different from my primary family's, and then those differences showed up in my relationship to Tom. This was the first time there was a connection and closeness to people that felt somewhat similar to me. They had many of the same concerns, plans, and interests. My whole body and mind relaxed with that knowledge.

Nothing good was happening for Tom and me, but there was a tiny spark of hope in my heart.

Cursillo

"We are not meant to stay wounded.
We are supposed to move through our tragedies and
challenges and to help each other move through the
many painful episodes of our lives."
—Caroline Myss

The Archbishop of St. Paul approached me and asked me to become the rector of a series of women's retreats in Minnesota with the goal of developing women church leaders. "Yes" was the answer I gave, and my biggest involvement for several years was the Cursillo.

What Cursillo means is "short course in Christianity." It started in Spain in 1944 and came to the United States in 1965. It started in the Catholic Church, but is now part of several religions. It continues to this day.

The Cursillo gave me a chance to use my speaking and creative skills. It taught me to create community. Each event brought together a Catholic priest and ten other team members to provide a learning and loving experience for forty women. It lasted four days, and I facilitated fourteen of these events.

The excitement, the planning, and the execution of the whole event was a highlight and brought me sincere joy. At one point, I was able to bring my mother to experience one of the events.

Again, however, my "inside" life and my "outside" life were miles apart. It was another extension of what I learned as a child.

On one of these weekends, toward the end of that leadership time, I had what I thought was a breakdown. Today I see it as a breakthrough.

The music was playing, and the attendees of the workshop then in progress were making collages and visiting around big round tables. I remember I was wearing a bright orange corduroy skirt and had just delivered a lecture on spirituality. Walking directly out of the room where they were working, I went to the shower, left my clothes on the floor and went inside and sobbed and sobbed. My heart was breaking.

The retreat was for a group of forty women who came to hear my team walk them through steps to help them search for authenticity and find ways to serve others in their lives.

My ability to design and offer a path to them was clear. My sobs resulted from knowing that my own path was blocked. The truth was that I was deeply stuck in my own life. The distance between what was most important to me (my own authenticity) and the reality of the breakdown in my life was huge. It was an ocean of emotional and physical pain.

The shower muffled the sound of my sobbing and the crying went on for a very long time. After about an hour, I made a resolution to myself to accept that my life in that moment had become unbearable. Promising myself to change whatever I could gave me the strength to come out of the shower. What I didn't have at that time was the know-how or the direction. It was only clear that changes had to be made, no matter what.

LESSONS LEARNED

I realized at a very deep level that my life had become so divided that there were two of me. I was the person whose creativity was at an all-time high and was full of compassion, inspiration, and desire to be with other people. I was the same person who went home at night and was rejected, and felt isolated and lonely. It was clear my life had to change radically in every way: spiritually, emotionally, and physically.

Time, Energy, and Money

"Your beliefs become your thoughts.
Your thoughts become your words.
Your words become your actions.
Your actions become your habits.
Your habits become your values.
Your values become your destiny."

—Mahatma Gandhi

Those fourteen, four-day women's retreats were life changing. My title was rector. For someone who wanted to be a priest, rector felt very good. My responsibility was to put together a team of ten women who shared their life stories with thirty other invited guests. It was about our faith and how we came to believe in God. It was such fun and so much learning and bonding. Today, I still connect with some of them.

My invitation went to each woman of my team. The invitations were based on my having observed their special gifts. Each was to present a talk, or "share," and design some kind of experiential workshop to share that talk. Each team presented one-tenth of the workshop, and every team member learned from nine other women. Then we invited the thirty other women to be part of the workshop.

The intent was for the team to provide a loving and caring experience for the thirty women, but truth be told, the team received as much and maybe more than it gave. The event was a pure gift both ways. The team decorated with flowers and color, chose great music, provided art materials, and led the inspiring program.

As women registered on Thursday night, we shared a pledge of silence until Friday morning. Having a transition time of silence between the rush of daily life and the beginning of a soul-searching four days was just the right decision. By Friday, there had been reflection, confusion, annoyance, relief, interest, and a deep calming down. Add to it a night of sleep and by Friday morning, everyone was ready to talk, share, and connect.

Friday was filled with lectures, personal stories, questions, art projects, and self-examination about many things: values, beliefs, dreams, loss, grief, relationships, history, the present, and the future. Friday felt like it was a week long. The intensity of self-examination was punctuated by music, art projects, and group feedback.

Saturday morning was more of the same. Saturday afternoon moved into ideas for solutions, processing of information, evaluation of group feedback, and making plans for how to use all the information that was presenting itself. By prearrangement, we had obtained letters of support from loved ones of our attendees. We had a mail call on Saturday and delivered these letters to our group. By Saturday night dinner, each attendee was bursting at the seams—or souls-feeling love, support, and inspiration. Each had her own personal story to feel, accept, and understand in new ways.

Sunday morning we were awakened by a live musical group that came to our beds and gave us songs, fresh flowers, and a message that "It was a new day and one more new beginning." As we went into a large room to begin the morning session, there was a curtain covering half the room. As the session progressed and feelings of hope, peace, and satisfaction permeated the air, the curtains opened. Sitting there were countless family members and friends showing up for brunch to welcome the attendees back into their daily lives. It was a spiritual and magical moment.

Being a part of these fourteen events changed me and changed my life. I never really felt alone again. My soul had learned to connect and I knew—and still know—that I can get myself into places and relationships that want to and will nourish me. I can also give that sense of belonging to someone else. In giving and receiving, I find connection and belonging.

The major lesson from these weekends was to evaluate where you put your time, money, and energy. You will then find where your value system is. Keep changing your time commitments, your money spent, and your energy released until those actions match what you say your value system is. I find this is a daunting and constant reevaluation; it makes me who I am, and keeps my actions true to my values.

Living life is like being in a small boat on an ocean. We have a choice. We fight each wave and resist until we tip over, or we can learn to go with the flow.

LESSONS LEARNED

My awakening and lesson was that there was reason to hope. Everything about the Cursillo spoke to me. My spirituality deepened. The faith that had been with me since I was a child blossomed. There was a return of the creativity and thinking that had been awakened by Mrs. Mett and Mr. Halos in high school. They had seen something in me that allowed me to trust myself and believe in myself; it was happening again.

I learned that time, energy, and money were indicators of what we believed in, and I knew that my life was changing, even if I did not know how. For the first time, there was thought of new action. Really liking myself and what I believed in was intoxicating.

Heartview Treatment Center

"Until we're all healed, no one is healed."
—Martin Luther King Jr.

During my crisis years with Tom, I tried every route I could to find Tom professional help. There were two issues going on for me at the same time, which compounded the problems. One was Tom's anger and hostility. His refusal to work as a couple was bringing me great stress. At the same time my mom's addictions (smoking and drinking) were taking their toll on me and my siblings. Of course our relationship was in real trouble, but I didn't realize how much my mom's issues affected me and, by extension, us.

Tom refused to reach out for any outside help, so my efforts were as a lone person. There were countless sessions with priests, counselors, psychologists, and psychiatrists, but to no avail. Eventually, once I went back to school, I became convinced that my coming from and being affected by my parents' alcoholism was a big part of my pain. Somehow I needed to find out more about addiction. This was a long time before information about alcoholism and the family illness of codependency was public.

One night at a dinner party, someone mentioned there was a new treatment center called Heartview in Mandan, North Dakota. They mentioned that they took almost anyone and felt they made healing progress. This was pure word of mouth, long before cell phones and the Internet. It felt like hope that came out of the blue.

A friend offered to care for my children. I knew her well and knew they would be well cared for. I took a bus for many hours and arrived at Heartview late at night. As I showed up at the door, a man answered my knock and said, "What the hell are you doing here?"

My words were that I was lonely, scared, ashamed, angry, and empty. His words were, "Which one of your parents drank?" My word was, "Both." He said, "Come in dear, we can help." I didn't drink, but I entered an alcoholism treatment center and found a recovery lifestyle that is with me today. My gratitude is very present. The twelve-step way of life is a good life and has proven so for millions of people. I am one of them.

After I completed the program I promised myself that, with God's help, someday there would be a place or a center that would welcome and treat family members and those for whom active alcoholism isn't the issue, but rather the equally serious family issues and other addictions. My promise to myself came true with the founding of Onsite Training and Consulting (now called Onsite Workshops), which offers the miracle of recovery and continues to this day in Tennessee. My life changed with my treatment experience. My recovery date is forty-plus years.

The treatment experience was much the same as many programs today. There were lectures, group therapy, reading, twelve-step meetings, informal sharing with others, and learning how to live one day at a time.

One of my lessons is that the program doesn't have to fit the expectations of the client or be perfect. There were fifty-plus people who were in treatment because they were addicts, and then there was me, the sole identified family member who didn't drink. What I also learned was how many addicts there were who had come from alcoholic families themselves.

My thirty-day stay in this program changed my life. It made me feel sane and my life made sense now that I knew more about my parents' addictions. My mission was to bring this information to other children of alcoholics— and find a way to help them.

LESSONS LEARNED

Heartview's greatest gift was to give me a voice to share all the pain of my childhood in an atmosphere of caring and listening. They were unsure about what to do with me, but they listened with love.

The other lifelong lesson from Heartview I learned was about the twelve-step way of life that is a core value for me to this day. My life would not be the same without it. Living the steps has brought me the promised serenity and wisdom of how to live each day.

Divorce from Tom

*"Somehow in many moments, and then finally in one moment,
I stood my ground instead of running away."*
—Sharon Wegscheider-Cruse

There was no going back. Worlds were colliding, and I asked Tom for a divorce on three occasions. He never put down the newspaper he was reading and he never answered me. The pain brought about numbness inside of me. I would drift through the days and the need to try again, asking for a divorce on a regular basis from March to September of that year.

Inside me a determination and focus were forming. Going to an attorney not known to me and making plans to have Tom served with divorce papers at work was one of the bravest and scariest things I had ever done. When he came home the night I had the papers served, he was full of rage but silent. I waited. Finally, in a few days he talked to me, furious that I had him served at work. Now, he needed to respond. He did.

We never fought about it or even talked very much about the divorce. He gave me two choices. One, I could leave without the children; he would keep them and support them. Or, two, I could take the children with me and he would not support them. It would be me and them without support. He knew I would never leave without them and believed I would stay in the marriage. The children and I left.

In the 1960's, the culture and law favored men. The judge said he had to pay something to finalize the divorce. He chose $100 a month for all three children. Once a month, I gave each child $33. That would never happen today. My heart had been broken, but I vowed that my children should never suffer. After thirteen years of marriage, I was left with forty dollars.

Sadness, a sense of guilt, and shame were growing in me. It was frightening to be so alone. By now, my dad had died, my best friend had died, and my mom was in deep addiction with alcohol and prescription pills. My children were precious, and yet it was clear they were afraid of what was going to happen to them. They were as powerless and threatened as I was in regard to leaving our home.

Again I was torn apart. On the inside there was so much guilt, shame, fear, and anxiety. On the outside, I was starting to take college classes and they were going very well. There was an increasing number of Cursillo retreats that brought me great joy and a sense of hope, and I loved raising my children. But on the inside, I was in turmoil.

The Caesar Salad Disaster

I just knew this night would be a bad one. My ex-husband Tom was never cooperative in any way. The divorce had been painful and the time leading up to the divorce even worse. I just didn't want to communicate with him about anything.

However, my children were the center and core of my life. Because I did not have enough money for college for our son, I needed to communicate with my ex-husband. I met him and his new wife in a restaurant that was a little upscale for my budget, but I so wanted this dinner to go well. I was ready to treat them to dinner. I was going to ask him to help pay for our son's education.

We met. My ex-husband ordered a prime rib dinner with all the fixings. His wife ordered a steak dinner with all the trimmings, and I ordered a Caesar salad. The waiter, dressed in black and looking very elegant, served my guests their salad, soup, and bread, and we started our dinner. I had asked the waiter to bring my salad with their entrees. The discussion began but did not go well. While my guests ate, they were letting me know that their new family would require all of their income and there was none left over for my son. I could not believe the ease with which they could eat dinner and refuse to help me or my son—his son too—in any way.

My feelings were escalating; my hurt was deep and my anger was rising. By the time they were ready to bring out the prime rib and steak, my insides felt like I had been on a merry-go-round at full speed.

The good-looking waiter returned with his Caesar salad cart and began his masterpiece. He rubbed the bowl with fresh garlic, wiped a lemon wedge inside, and then began the salad dressing. Each little spice was added one at a time, then came the lettuce, crisp and wrapped in a damp cotton towel. Finally the tiny slivers of anchovies were gently folded in. By now, my guests were in the middle of their entrees.

When the waiter finished his masterpiece, tears were burning in my eyes. I asked him to "Put it in a box to go." He looked completely crestfallen and said, "Are you sure?" and I said, "Completely sure." I took my salad and left, leaving the guests to their own bill. I left determined to pay for college for my son and myself. It was a joint effort. My son earned scholarships. He did go to college and even got a master's degree.

LESSONS LEARNED

What I learned in my time with Tom is that too often two people marry long before they work out the issues of their family of origin. When I married, I was still almost a child and in no position to choose a life mate. My family of origin was in crisis, and in some deep place, I was looking for safety and security. I was not choosing a lifetime mate. I did all that was expected of a young wife and none of it worked. We were not bad people, just very much not compatible with each other.

The best thing that Tom and I did was to choose to have three children that I treasure today. Tom had his own relationship with each of them and that is their story. He was an intelligent, good-intentioned, and faithful person. They have each inherited his best qualities.

I learned that I needed a very different lifestyle than we could have had together. From the bottom of my heart I believe my children are better because of our divorce. Somehow I learned at a deep level that all connections with Tom were over for me.

Chapter Four

EVOLUTION

College

*"Information without action leads to frustration
and depression. Experience life with a focus;
do not just drift through it."*

—Sharon Wegscheider-Cruse

I had started college and was in training to be a counselor specializing in addiction studies. I was also learning how seriously damaged I was in my painful family system.

College for me was the most thrilling thing I had ever done except to give birth. Being a student and a mom and a retreat leader kept me going for years. My ex-husband, however, became more and more rigid, controlling, and in many ways emotionally cruel. He was connected to me because he was the father of my children. My lifestyle, my family of origin, my church, and my frame of reference all suggested to me that this was my lot in life. At that time I was in my thirties.

As my children grew, it became very clear to me that if my unhappiness was because of my former marriage and the circumstances in which I lived, then my children's lives were going to be affected as well. When living conditions got to the point that I felt my children were being shortchanged and exposed to behavior that was not going to be to their benefit as they grew, I went into a terrible depression.

During this whole time, I was living three lives. One was the "life at home," the second was my "Cursillo life," and the third was my "college life." I finished college; it took me nine full years, but I completed undergraduate and graduate degrees, as well as certifications in both addiction and psychodrama.

LESSONS LEARNED

Not going to college right out of high school was a good move for me. The appreciation I felt at this stage of my life about getting to go to college was overwhelming in the best way possible.

Every class, every professor, and every experience was golden. Being a good student came naturally; maybe life experience had something to do with it. English and speech were a snap, and business was exciting and I adapted well. The only thing that slowed me down was having to inject rats with drugs. I could have skipped that part, but it was so life saving and changing to learn so much about alcoholism. This was my personal life I was learning about.

Friendship Club

*"If you want others to be happy, practice compassion.
If you want to be happy, practice compassion."*
—The Dalai Lama

During my years of Cursillo retreats and going to college, there was much creativity, music, and community building. It was healing for me, and I felt the desire to have something similar for young people. My children deserved to heal and have joy in their lives too.

There was a church in the inner city of Minneapolis that had a charismatic priest. He was especially gifted in working with those in need. He was well known in Minneapolis and church circles.

He led a church that specialized in human interest groups and programs. I went to him and asked if there would be space in his church for me to start a program for young and older children to bring them community and point them in a direction much like I was finding in the Cursillo movement. He said yes and I formed several groups according to age and facilitated them. I went to local women's groups and schools' internship programs and asked if I could use some of their women and young men to help me facilitate these groups. The Friendship Club was formed and we met for about two years.

My hope was that this socially conscious priest would donate space and let me put together a young adult community and then my children could be part of it.

The church gave me a finished basement, where I began leading groups of children from five to fifteen. As that happened, I noticed that some children could come together and share and mix with the group, while others could not. They were too frozen emotionally to enter into a relationship with me or the other children. I tried to meet with their parents. The apparently

better-adjusted children's parents were eager to meet, but the parents of the children who seemed to be emotionally hurting avoided any contact. This made me very curious. My children were a part of these groups and we had this special time together.

Later, I went to schools and asked if I could cross-check what I was learning by personally observing some students in grade schools, middle schools, and high schools. I found out that children filled different roles in all levels of schooling. There were the students who excelled in academics or sports, who I named the *family heroes*; there were those that spent a great deal of time in trouble—in the principals' offices or absent. I called them the *scapegoats*. Then there were the quiet ones who just were somewhat in the group backgrounds—in glee club and band, etc. To me they seemed like *lost children*, so that's what I named them. Lastly, there were the silly ones demanding attention. I called them the *mascots*.

Each of these roles broke down into two sub-groups. There were those that used this behavior in some kind of defense role, yet they could be helped to let go of their role and become more open in many ways. For them, it was stressful and scary to change, but with help and support, they could. Then there were others who were very fixed and could not change out of their role. They were highly rigid and very emotionally pained. They had lost their ability to choose.

I wanted to investigate why this was so and asked the officials at the schools if I could meet with their parents at the parent conferences. This was most eye-opening. First of all, many of the parents with children who were most resistant did not attend parent conferences, and of those that did, they were primarily female. Through careful questioning, the interviews suggested that one of the parents had a drinking problem. These roles that I had identified eventually formed a key part of my teaching and writing. (Much more to come on that.)

I continued that research by personal observation and found that the children in fixed pain were living in alcoholic or drug-abusing homes. Many of the mothers had suffered some kind of cancer, most often breast cancer. Asthma was prevalent in this group of children; one or both parents were often smokers. The time frame for all this hands-on investigation was the seventies.

It was a very successful adventure. It was while meeting as a volunteer in the Friendship Group that it became clear to me that young people fell into two very defined groups. There were those that showed behavior that told me they were from very happy homes. Their personalities showed many similar traits. They had authentic achievement skills, connected easily with others, shared their feelings, and were generally happy kids. Then there were the other young people who were more afraid and quick to anger, needed to draw attention to themselves, and were perfectionistic. Some were very distracting to the group as a whole by using humor in inappropriate ways.

It was the beginning of my doing research on these children and eventually making the link to alcoholic homes. It was the rough beginning of my knowing that children from alcoholic or painful families developed traits different from children from healthy homes.

It became clear that these children needed help. I felt it was important to take what I had learned from the Friendship Club and use it to create a program. That was the beginning of the Family Factory.

LESSONS LEARNED

From the Friendship Club I learned compassion not only for the children we were working with, but for myself. It would have been so wonderful to have a group like this while growing up. Intellectually, I learned many things, but emotionally, my frequent tears taught me there was still emotional pain.

University Years: The Sixties

"I need to focus on today. Some things are
over and done with. History cannot be rewritten.
Action needs to take place."

—Sharon Wegscheider-Cruse

Not going to college right after high school made me very sad. That's where my friends were headed and I loved to learn. High school had been a fulfilling adventure for me and I wanted more. However, it was not in my destiny.

Today there would be school counselors, interested families, ways to seek scholarships, student loans, and a plethora of possibilities. Those resources were not there for me in 1956. My family had lost everything through fire, addiction, and poor health. Getting a job and helping my family was uppermost in my reality.

Now with my grown-up awareness, I realize that if I had gone to college in the fifties, I would have missed one of the most significant eras for college students. I was involved in nine years of college in the sixties. That era helped shape my thinking, my vision, my path, and my values. Being in college at that time was part of my destiny.

Having the opportunity to learn made me giddy with joy. It felt like much of my life had been in black and white; now it was living color. Themes expanded, awareness was sharper, and there were constant value choices to be made. The political and social upheaval was something our country had never experienced.

My curriculum included four quarters of black culture. The fifties version of women only as homemakers was blowing up day by day, and I suddenly realized that two young men I went to high school with were really a couple.

It was as though a lens cleared up my vision and fog. Clarity was becoming a new realization each day.

A president was shot, black leaders were shot, and presidential candidates were shot. Betty Friedan was writing brand-new information for me in her book, *The Feminine Mystique*, and Gloria Steinem was saying things I felt but would never have said out loud. Marlo Thomas was showing a nation of women a whole different kind of role model on *That Girl*, the television series in which she starred. My world was being turned upside down.

My role had always been to be a good daughter, a good student, a good wife, and a good mother. Rarely was there any thought about myself and my own needs, and certainly not my wants. There were dreams, excitements, learning, and adventures stored inside me for more than twenty-six years. Maybe not even at a conscious level. With all the chaos of the world situations, my thinking and feeling were waking up. My only constant was my deep love for my children. Little did I know that in a few years, my love for my children and my learning and going to school would collide and become the basis for a very successful career. (Lots more to come on that, too.)

Meanwhile, the sixties continued to shock us all. Even though being a wife and mother was my primary occupation, it was natural and fitting to form an identity and become part of the idealism of college students during this time of upheaval to our history. We did believe we could "make a difference" and change the world. As a group, we felt responsible and accountable. We had a deep need to cry out and work for justice, understanding, and equality.

I was proud to become a feminist. I had already learned in high school that I could have a voice and deliver a message. When I got to college, it felt necessary to show up, stand up, and speak my truth. I was shocked to find out that it *did* matter. My voice was heard in college circles, where people were protesting the Vietnam War and racial inequality, women's rights and gender equality. One of my close friends was a draft card burner who made national headlines. Going to visit him in prison was my first experience with the legal system.

LESSONS LEARNED

The sixties were an eye-opening time to be in college. There were protests, marches, and unrest. It wasn't just about classes and ordinary college happenings.

I learned about racism, sexism, protests, and feminism, and many of the lessons were experiential. I wore one pair of jeans for two years, but because I lived in the suburbs, mine were washed and ironed daily. My suburban neighbors thought I was different. Eventually, I quit playing bridge and started volunteering at food shelters instead.

My values were being challenged, and my actions needed to fit my values.

Family Time with Don

*"They say a person needs just three things to be
truly happy in this world: someone to love, something to do,
and something to hope for."*

—Tom Bodett

During the years that I worked with Cursillo, I developed a friendship
with the spiritual director. He was a Catholic priest and was in his own crisis
about whether to stay in the priesthood. He had taken a long sabbatical and
lived in Germany for a while as he came to terms with what was happening in
the church and the culture of the sixties. He returned from Europe knowing
that he needed to leave the priesthood.

His leaving the priesthood and my leaving my marriage took place in the
same time frame. We had become friends during the time of the Cursillo
work; our work together was intoxicating and fulfilling. We both were on
track to become counselors, and we had a great deal in common. We were
both children from alcoholic families and both felt we were on a mission. He
asked me to marry him and I said, "Yes."

There was a relief beyond description. We loved each other and were both
excited about our work. We both loved my children and the home life we created was good. Though we worked for different agencies, we did similar work.

His name was Don and he was a very social person. It was such a relief
after living around such anger and tension most of the time. As a family, we
did many things. We went camping and had fun with friends. We had not
done that before. This was healing for all of us in many ways. We traveled and
visited Hawaii, and for the first time I felt like we had a family.

Our marriage had a couple of challenges right from the beginning. One
was that we were both public people because of the Cursillo. By then our

network had grown to about 2,000 people, and for the two leaders to have made such drastic decision was not well accepted in the community. Some people understood and were kind to us; others were not. Some are still good friends today.

The other difficulty is that divorce was uncommon in the sixties. Being children of divorce was not easy for my children; sometimes they were the only ones in their class to have divorced parents. This was a hard time for them but I did the best I could.

Don was a good father to my children. There were all kinds of feelings that we had to navigate, but we remained a close family as best we could.

We had lots of young people in and out of our house. My children had many sleepovers and I closed my eyes when they wanted to make chocolate-chip cookies and spaghetti—in the middle of the night. We took many trips. One daughter, her friend, and I drove to Nashville to hear the Grand Ole Opry. Both my daughters got involved with Timber Bay, a Christian youth group.

On Friday nights when the workweek was finished, I would pack up the kids and take them to a local hotel where we could all have supper together. Then they could swim in the hotel pool. We would stay overnight and would go home the next morning.

Every Tuesday night, we would eat at an inexpensive steak house near our home. It was well known, so it felt like a special outing. We would have steak, potato, and salad for $2.35. We brought our own Heinz 57 and felt we were "upscale" having steak once a week.

We also rotated cooking meals at home, with each child taking a turn. Patrick made spaghetti, Sandy made lasagna, and Debbie made macaroni and cheese. Tuesday was steak, the hotel was Friday night, Don took a night, and I took a night. Our meals were predictable and good. It was good family time.

We did not watch much TV, only special shows. We played many games and had fun together.

For fourteen months at a time, we brought students in from a foreign exchange program. Our students came from Finland, France, Germany, Sweden, Japan, and, for a shorter time, Mexico. We had a pop-up trailer and went camping as many weekends as we could. Often one of my girlfriends and her children would go during the week and our husbands would join us on the weekends. Looking back, I know I did my best to bring a social life and connection into the lives of my children. My career was beginning to be demanding—by now I was working at the Johnson Institute, an intervention center in Minnesota—but I always knew my kids came first.

LESSONS LEARNED

In my new relationship with Don there were many lessons.

Right away I knew what it was like to lose many friends overnight because of our decision to marry. We were leaders in the Catholic Church, which frowns upon divorce. Don had made the decision to leave the priesthood much earlier, so people didn't get as upset with him for that. But it was hard to be the woman, a divorcée, whom he chose to marry. In my heart, I knew I had done the right thing to divorce, but the lesson I learned is that it was just too hard for many Catholics to accept.

The other lesson I learned is that family life is possible. Don was wonderful to my children even though he was day and night different from Tom. Don and I often talked about that wide gap. He showed us what it was like to have someone who was engaged with the family. He was good for us, and my family brought him joy as well.

Nurturing Networks, Inc.

"Success is where preparation and
opportunity meet."
—Bobby Unser

With all the chaos and change in the world, the way I managed my role in it was to write. Small booklets were my first attempt. I had been teaching part time at the University of Minnesota, and students wanted my ideas in written form. Not being able to afford the number of handouts I needed, I found a small printing company that put my original material in small booklets and sold them to the students. They got passed around and people starting ordering them in bulk. I decided to form a small, for-profit distribution company.

Teaching at the University of Minnesota in the Public Health department was beginning to get expensive. There were several students and I used many handouts. Since it was beginning to be a financial hardship, my idea was to take those handouts, put them in little booklets of about twenty to forty pages, and use those as handouts for the course. I found a printer who could do that for me and I could cover my cost plus add another fifty cents as profit. When I bought them in bulk, he gave me an even better price and there I was—in business. I copyrighted my handout ideas and started selling these booklets to my classes.

My distribution company was incorporated as Nurturing Networks. Money was going out and only some was coming back. It was a beginning time. Don and I were struggling both emotionally and financially. Yet it was always clear that my motives and passion were pure. By now, it was evident to me that God wanted me to use my gifts to follow a mission. So many angels had been put in my path and the directions were very much laid out for me. There was just enough income coming in to hold on and see what would happen.

The orders started coming in. The first few were from individuals and I mailed them out. The next orders were from treatment centers, counselors, schools, and businesses, and it became necessary to hire more employees. The first two were my daughters, Sandy and Debbie; they were handling orders of several hundred to five thousand copies. When my son came home from college on a visit, he helped me buy our first computer, a Kaypro. It cost $5,000. We had a bona fide business.

We were operating as a mail-order business. My daughters cleverly handled phone orders. When a call came in, one daughter would answer and refer the caller to the order department. The other daughter would pick up the phone. Once the order was taken, she would refer back to the shipping department, the first daughter. There were many departments, and many calls transferred between the two. They did a great job.

Nurturing Networks produced many booklets and sold thousands. It provided housing and expenses for my girls during their college years. Both girls learned a skill and entrepreneurial flair; they knew financial management and business. As adults, both are intelligent, skilled, and know how to get things done. Nurturing Networks taught us all many lessons.

Eventually, I put all those booklets together and began publishing books with two great publishers: Science and Behavior of Palo Alto, California, and Health Communications of Deerfield Beach, Florida.

Virginia Satir always told me, "Be yourself. You will always be a second-class copy of anyone else, but a first-class original for yourself." I think she was so right.

LESSONS LEARNED

I learned that what I was developing in regard to families and recovery had value. People wanted information. My confidence was growing.

The next big learning was how to set up a business. My accountant was a sage for me as he helped me set up my first corporation. Earning money for a product I produced was a new experience. Write once, and money comes in again and again through distribution. This was another important learning. Until now, each exchange had needed input. This was not quite passive income, but it was ongoing money for a one-time effort. Learning all about distribution became the next hurdle.

Healing in My Thirties

*"Faith is trusting that things can be different even if
the evidence does not bear that out."*

—Sharon Wegscheider-Cruse

These were golden years for me, but they were hard years for my children. For me, it was the first stable family that I had ever experienced. My Cursillo work was satisfying, and my work with children in the Friendship Club was teaching me so much about family systems. Since divorce was not common in the sixties, however, it was hard for my children to be from what people referred to as a "broken family." That term was repugnant to me, since this was the first family system that had ever worked for me.

There wasn't much financial security in my life. My mom was in her addiction and that was still painful. My husband had taken a vow of poverty in the Catholic Church, so he started from scratch when he left the priesthood. My work was more about the discoveries I was making through my hands-on research and there was not a great deal of money.

However, each year we scraped together enough money for a trip to Disneyland or Walt Disney World.

LESSONS LEARNED

I learned ways of living that brought me healing in my thirties. There was a balance of working in the Cursillo, Family Factory, Nurturing Networks, and the Friendship Club. I learned to balance output with input and having time with my family was important.

I learned from my children who were still growing up. Regardless of how little money we had, we made it to Disneyland or Walt Disney World on a regular basis, and we made many memories there.

Disneyland and Walt Disney World

"When you believe in a thing, believe in
it all the way, implicitly and unquestionably.
If you can dream it, you can do it."

—Walt Disney

Disneyland and Disney World have played a huge role in my family's lives. It started with the first trip to California to see Disneyland when we camped nearby in orange groves and everything was new and awesome. Until we got there, the closest we had come was the Sunday night "Walt Disney's Wonderful World of Color" TV show. After watching each show open with the shot of Main Street and Cinderella's castle at the end of the street, actually walking down Main Street and heading to the castle was truly magical.

Several times my children and I went to California, where we came to know the Magic Kingdom inside out. Some years, the song "It's a Small World," stayed in our heads for weeks at a time. As a family, we bonded at Disneyland.

Then came the magical moment when Disney World opened in Florida and the amazement of Epcot (Experimental Prototype of the Community of Tomorrow). By now we were taking grandchildren as well and some of my whole three-generational family; good times were to be had in the land of magic. We have camped in Fort Wilderness, tried many of the on-campus resorts, and done all the rides and exhibits countless times. Many times these visits were the glue that held our family together during tough times.

The first of two favorite memories is taking my children there shortly after my divorce. To save money, we decided we would drive our VW van, take our own gear, and rent a tent site at Fort Wilderness when we got there. That was

how I planned to spend our Christmas; I thought they'd be thrilled. Everyone was allowed one suitcase and the rest was camping gear.

The first adventure along the way came just before Chicago, when I discovered that my son was under a blanket listening to music that had nothing to do with the radio. He had somehow rigged up a radio system of his own with batteries and two speakers, taking up more than his share of our gear space. To top it off, while showing me what he had rigged up, I saw something silver under another the blanket. He confessed that he thought that it wouldn't be Christmas without a tree, so he had smuggled a silver Christmas tree into the gear space.

By the time we got to Chicago, a snowstorm forced us off the roads into a motel. Finally, as the snowstorm continued to rage, it was clear there would be no driving to Florida. The only way we could get to Orlando in a reasonable amount of time and salvage our plans would be to fly—something for which I certainly didn't have the money, which is why we were driving and camping. It was a big, difficult decision, but I took a leap of faith and decided to fly, putting the tickets on a credit card, which I knew would take months to pay off. I asked the motel manager if we could leave our van there for two weeks. He agreed and arranged a shuttle ride for us to O'Hare Airport, which was still open. We left all our gear in the van, and took our suitcases and the silver Christmas tree.

Since we couldn't afford plane tickets and a hotel room—even on credit— we called Fort Wilderness and explained what had happened and how we couldn't take our gear; they told us to come anyway. They had other cancellations due to Midwest storms and would figure something out. We arrived late that night, suitcases and tree in hand. For the price of a campsite, they gave us a fully equipped Airstream Motor Home for the next two weeks. It was an amazing vacation! Some angel somewhere was looking out for us.

The second favorite memory was taking the grandchildren to Cinderella Castle for a story about Little Red Riding Hood. All the children, aged three to six, were sitting in a group on the floor, with the adults standing around that circle. Cinderella was telling her story and came to the part where Little Red Riding Hood brought her picnic basket to her grandma. She asked the grandkids what they thought Grandma would like in her basket. My five-year-old granddaughter waved her hand in the air and when Cinderella chose her, she said, "My grandma would like a glass of cold chardonnay." Out of the mouths of babes!

It was never about the mouse. It was about the whole family coming together and having fun. We have found other ways to have fun, but Disney owns a corner of our hearts—and a chunk of my bank account!

LESSONS LEARNED

Disney and its philosophy taught my family and me many important lessons about family togetherness, finding adventures, and trying new things. It isn't about the mouse or the corporate venture. The lessons are around what families can do together there. Something is always available for every age and interest. Then when we get back together again, there is sharing, laughter, and joy. My family and I have hundreds of Disney stories that will stay with us forever. It's a glue that binds our family stories together in many ways.

The Family Factory

"Believe in yourself. Have faith in your abilities.
Without a humble but reasonable confidence in your own
powers, you cannot be successful or happy."

—Norman Vincent Peale

I devoted quite a lot of time and effort to the Cursillo, and it was very satisfying to see it have such a strong, positive influence in the community. In many ways working in and for the church was also very good for me; it preserved my sanity and allowed some sort of creativity to flow through me. My children were always foremost in my mind. Having something like the Cursillo with its music, sense of belonging, creativity, and joy for young people, motivated me to start a similar movement and program. I wanted a real therapy center for youngsters.

There was no money to do so, and it took many creative moves to get one started. The success of the volunteer Friendship Club program encouraged me to start a real therapy center. When my first agency took shape, I named it "The Family Factory." The family consisted of many parts, and so did the people in the family. The idea was to put the parts in working order. This was all happening in 1972 and 1973.

To attract leaders, invitations were given to volunteers, the Junior League women's group, interns from my college, and anyone else who cared about young people. Soon, there were about fifty young people meeting every other week. Within three months, there were almost 100 people from grade school and junior high participating.

The volunteers and I were the only ones in the beginning running The Family Factory. School was finished for me, and by then I was a single parent, and the first and only paid employee. My children supported me by eating many a hot dog meal or apples and popcorn. Because this work was so important to me, we got by with a nominal charge for the groups. Because the children were showing such remarkable progress, the groups grew and grew.

A woman in recovery from alcoholism volunteered to be the receptionist. Even buying two phone lines was a stretch in those days. She was a great receptionist if one line rang. If two lines rang, she became overwhelmed and cried. But she hung on for the life of that first agency.

We were housed in an H&R Block income-tax building that was donated to me by a recovering alcoholic, but we could only have it from May to February. He needed it for tax business mid-February through April. When he needed it for taxes, we would suspend the program and resume again when we could. Obviously, this was a very shoestring operation.

LESSONS LEARNED

What I learned from setting up my first agency was almost more than can be recorded here. First, I was responsible for everything. There was no one to look to, ask questions of, or to help me. It was a one-person happening. There were no set hours, no salaries, no benefits, no technology, or free weekends.

The second thing I learned was that freedom could be exhilarating; my agency could be anything that I wanted it to be. The Family Factory also gave me a chance to do hands-on research that couldn't have happened any other way.

Developing a second corporation gave me a great deal of confidence personally and professionally.

The House

"Generosity is giving more than you can and
pride is taking less than you need."

—Khalil Gibran

The Family Factory programs were bursting at the seams. Our space was limited. We had so many children under the age of sixteen that our H&R Block tax building was full all the time.

I appealed to the Johnson Institute in Minneapolis, which finally let us use their building at night since they were a nine-to-five operation. Our groups could then start at 7:00 PM. We held groups every night. One would meet from 6:30 PM until 8:00 PM, and the second from 8:00 PM to 9:30 PM. These were adult children of alcoholics groups. They ran for a very nominal fee and my group leaders worked for a very minimum wage. It was more of a spiritual mission than a part-time job. Once a month on a Saturday, I would facilitate a therapeutic intensive program, called a reconstruction. A reconstruction is a fourteen-hour intensive experiential psychodrama of one person's whole life. The focus is on exploring and then doing intensive (both intellectual and emotional release) therapy with one person (called the star) with a group of people adding a real life feel to the journey by role-playing the important people in that person's life. This process can range from twenty to forty people involved. It's a combination of role play, trauma expression, understanding, celebrating the meaningful events and allowing this star to re-experience their past and their present in order to make plans for a healthier future. It originated with Virginia Satir, and I added my own new pieces to the process (with her blessing).

It was while we were at the H&R Block building that the *Minneapolis Star* newspaper ran an article on this new idea of treating families of alcoholics.

About a week later, I received a call from a Pastor Nerin, from a very large Lutheran church in a suburb of Minneapolis.

He told me that he had a massive parking lot on the property and that right in the middle of it was a two-story house with a finished basement. The church was preparing to tear it down for additional parking, but he had talked to his board of directors and they agreed that giving it to me for a counseling center was a better mission for the church. It was an outright gift for as long as I wanted it.

My heart skipped a few beats. My children and young adults would have a home. I met with him within a couple of days and learned about a few of the conditions. The church would continue to own the building and pay all utilities. We agreed we would not hold programs on Sunday when they needed all of the space in the parking lot. He would choose a board of eight directors who would manage the building, I would become a board member, and lastly, I would give the Sunday sermon one Sunday a month to acquaint the parishioners with the programs at the house. We shook hands on the deal.

There were so many improvements they wanted to make to the house first, so we had a couple of months of daily contact as these were made. We painted the stairs to the lower area with messages and icons for children. The upstairs had four rooms perfect for groups, and the main floor became offices and a waiting room. The house underwent a major renovation. By the time we were ready to launch our opening, we had talked about the house so often that we incorporated and named the center "The House."

The board of directors were a fine group of people. We had the local police chief, a psychiatrist, an accountant, the pastor, a businessman, a teacher, a firefighter, and me. I was named the executive director. Over the years we helped so many people through individual counseling during the day and many groups at night. These were very successful years.

Professionally, they were wonderful years. During this time that I was able to make regular trips to learn about and explore all that was available to help families.

LESSONS LEARNED

What I learned about pure generosity and the loving values of kind people. Here was a church that did not know me or my work. They saw someone struggling to bring programs to children and families. After simply reading about my efforts, they gave up their plans for a parking area and remodeled and outfitted a house for us. This pure gift gave hope and help to many families over the years.

The board members' expertise covered all fronts, and they all gave time and money to make "The House" happen.

My Search for Virginia Satir

"Prepare the umbrella before it rains,
life is full of surprises!"
—Malay Proverb

In college, the information that made the most sense to me was the work of Virginia Satir, a well-known and well-respected pioneer in family therapy. This was before she had published any of her books, and of course there was no Internet. I searched and searched but simply could not find her. From time to time, I would try and then give up again. This went on about two years. However, the universe had other plans for me.

The names Salvador Minuchin, Gregory Bateson, Murray Bowen, and Milton Erickson were all familiar. Studying their work was interesting and productive, but it didn't spark the curiosity and aliveness I felt when working with families. Then one day I was given a two-page handout with the basis of the work of Virginia Satir. *Bam!* It was like she was living in my experience and explaining it fully and absolutely right on. My excitement grew as I used some of her ideas in my work, and I knew I had to find her and study with her.

One night on the way home from teaching at the university, I had a flat tire in a rainstorm. I didn't know what to do, but waiting in the car on a dark lonely street was getting me nowhere. Looking up and down the street, I saw one house with lights on, and I ran through the rain and rang the doorbell. A lovely woman came to the door and invited me in to use their phone to call for help. She made me hot chocolate while I waited. She and her husband were sitting at the kitchen table, filling out papers to go to Canada to a workshop with Virginia Satir.

I wanted to go too, but they explained it was impossible. Canada provided training for therapists through their government, and there was no way for an outsider to pay or register. They were citizens of Canada just spending some time in Minnesota. I took the phone number and called the workshop coordinators in Saskatchewan and they confirmed the same information.

I did my best to explain how badly I needed to attend but they said no. I called every day for at least three weeks. Finally they said, "Okay, come to the weeklong event, we will send you registration materials, but don't say anything to anyone about where you live. Just do not call us again!" I was thrilled. Now, how to get there?

At this time I was a single parent. Money was very tight. But there was an older man I knew who had been a colonel in the army. He lived in a shelter for recovering alcoholics. We became friends when I volunteered there. He missed his young grandchildren who were in another city, so I occasionally invited him for supper. He liked to play games with my children. My dad had died, so they were missing a grandpa.

At my house one night, I told him my plight and how I was trying to get to Canada. He left later and, while I was picking up our games, I noticed a piece of paper on the couch: it was a check for a few hundred dollars. That money ended up being within a few dollars of what my airfare and hotel bill came to. He also left a note: "Take what you learn and pass it on." A good friend volunteered to care for my children, and I was off to meet Virginia Satir. We became friends, personally and professionally.

LESSONS LEARNED

While I was searching for Virginia, I learned to be persistent, to focus, and to be willing to take a risk. Nothing had surfaced during my research in libraries and textbooks. None of the other students I called found anything, and my professors had no clue how to find her. My pursuit was in its second year before my break with the flat tire. My second lesson was that when the universe is ready, it finds a way for dreams to come true. Having my kids' "military" grandpa come through with the funds was a true, unexpected miracle.

Virginia Satir, My Professional Sage

"I have found I am a little bit of all that has happened to me.
Virginia was a game changer in my life."

—Sharon Wegscheider-Cruse

While I was working at The House, Virginia called me and asked me to make a film with her. She would do a fourteen-hour film with me in a reconstruction of my childhood.

After working for fourteen hours on the pain and dysfunction of my historical family, I then walked through the gifts of that same family. One way or another, my life had been intertwined with this group of people for forty years.

We role-played what it was like for my mom and dad to grow up. We went through the war years when my dad was a soldier. I saw in role-play what it was like for my mom to become pregnant with me. She was just a child, only eighteen. My parents had very difficult lives in those days of the Depression and war. They too battled with what it was like to live in families of poverty and alcoholism.

I was born in the Great Depression to people of love, but also people of need. It helped me to know about their history. Then we came forward and I had a chance to relive my younger years. Virginia and the role players gave me a voice I often did not have as a child. I was able to voice what I needed and wanted, and see how it might have been different if it could have been.

Virginia helped me take a good look at my connections in this fourteen-hour marathon. Then came her wise words.

As I started to integrate all that I had just been through, it was a bit overwhelming. I stared at all the role players that had been part of this psychodrama. She gently turned me around, insisted that I look into those clear and piercing blue eyes of hers, and said:

"Always remember that you are not turning your back on them. You are just going in a new direction. As you look at me, tell me how you are feeling." My answer? "Ready."

My life was never the same. It became possible for me to choose the life I wanted and needed. I did not have to stay stuck in ways that were taught to me as a child. I could forge my own path. I took this gift to heart, went in a different direction, and nothing has been the same. As singer-songwriter Jerry Florence, lead singer in the "Go With the Flow" vocal group, used to sing to me, "I love myself, just the way I am." I can now sing that song to myself.

Many years later, in 1984, Virginia came to our house in Palm Desert, California and spent an evening with my dear friends, all leaders in the addiction field. She did a private workshop. I took her to the Betty Ford Center in Rancho Mirage, and she so appreciated learning about addiction. It was an issue in her family that she had never talked about before. We remained close friends until her death in 1986. She wrote me a letter, which remains one of my treasures.

Letter from Virginia Satir to Sharon, 1977

In writing this letter of recommendation for Sharon Wegscheider, I feel a deep sense of privilege. Sharon has worked in-depth with me in seminars on several occasions, spanning about eight years. I have also worked with her collaboratively at the Johnson Institute.

I feel like I know Sharon very well. Much of that is due to her willingness to let herself be known.

I am impressed with her ability to learn, to conceptualize, to plan, to live out her plans sensitively and realistically, and to change directions if new conditions warrant it.

I trust Sharon implicitly. For me, this means that I know she knows what she knows, she knows when she doesn't know, and she is aware of the fact that she can be in the place where she doesn't know she doesn't know, which she handles by being open to feedback, both negative and positive, from the outside.

She has tremendous ability to sense what is going on in herself and others. Her ability to love fully accompanies an ability to let people stand on their own feet.

She is an original thinker and an innovator. This may be somewhat immodest of me to say; however, I feel she is one of the few persons I have met who match me in energy, ability to dream, and to be realistic, and in addition to be a fantastic risk taker. An example of her risk taking is the fact that she allowed herself to be filmed doing her family reconstruction. The film, called A Family Reconstruction, *is available for teaching and inspirational purposes.*

Judging from own experience, Sharon is a person who can turn the world on, sometimes at the expense of herself. I am in the process of learning. She may have gone beyond me.

Sincerely,

Virginia Satir

LESSONS LEARNED

Where would I ever begin to talk about lessons from Virginia? They are sprinkled throughout this book, but if I had to summarize, I would say I learned self-care, boundaries, and self-acceptance.

She re-parented me in many ways and filled in all the missing places left by parts of my childhood. One of her daughters once said to me, "I wish I had the same relationship with my mom that you had with her. She wasn't trying to hurt me in any way. It's just the way she saw it." Virginia once told me it was like we shared the same childhood and younger life and helped each other move on. I loved her.

The Esalen Institute

*"And the day came when the risk to remain tight in a bud
was more painful than the risk it took to blossom."*

—Anaïs Nin

In the sixties and seventies, the place to be for those seeking enlightenment and personal growth was the Esalen Institute in Big Sur, California. Esalen sits on the West Coast about as far as you can go and clings to a cliff. It is full of energy, unconventional ideas, and eclectic people. My first trip was with twelve male psychiatrists. It was an explosion of thought and feelings. It was a very long way—intellectually, emotionally, and personally—from my conservative childhood and adulthood. Listening to every word and trying every experience, my heart, soul, and consciousness began to change.

My studies were with Michael Murphy (one of Esalen's co-founders), Gabrielle Roth, Sam Keen, Ida Rolf, Richard Alpert (now Ram Dass), George Leonard, Will Schutz, Ilana Rubinfield, and an associate of Fritz Perls, the founder of Gestalt therapy. Even though it was all new to me, I absorbed and honored everything. I could learn and became close to many of the leaders during that time. They even invited me to come back and speak about conventional spirituality. They were most interested in my work in the Cursillo.

All in all, over time, I spent fourteen weeks at Esalen. I studied Gestalt, psychodrama, yoga, Rolfing, sports medicine, synergy, and countless ways to facilitate groups and build community. This was the time of the human potential movement, and I was in the middle of it all.

One of my favorite stories at that time was the hot-tub story. Knowing in advance that discussions and sharing stories in the hot tub were a well-known aspect of Esalen, I packed my black one-piece bathing suit. At the end of the first evening as people were leaving dinner, they mentioned to me, "See you at the tubs tonight." When it turned dark, I started along the lighted path to the edge of the cliff where candlelight was flickering through the entry to the hot tub area. Going in I saw many people in the tubs, their bathrobes hanging on hooks along one side. The other side was flickering with candles that were lit and positioned into the wall. It was magical.

Suddenly, my heart began to pound: everyone was nude. No bathing suits to be seen. The tubs were all down the center of the room, and on the ocean side were beautiful white tables where massages were to follow the hot-tub experience.

I was a bit uncomfortable with all these happy and laughing naked adults. Not wanting to draw attention to myself, I hung up my bathrobe and proceeded to the first of many hot tubs. As I began to get in, the people already there urged me on, saying, "When in Rome . . ." They assured me that it was a much better experience without a bathing suit.

Choice time. I stepped back, went over to the hook, stepped out of my bathing suit, hung it up on the hook, and stepped into the tub. The next thing I remembered was waking up on one of the massage tables with a group of people standing around telling me, "You are okay, you just fainted." The combination of the heat and the stress must have been too much. My attempt to not draw attention to myself had backfired. The next night, I found it was not a big deal to go without a suit.

LESSONS LEARNED

Many lessons were learned at Esalen. Each teacher had his or her own vision of what a "healthy and free individual" looked like. I experienced many of the people who have gone on to become legacies in their fields and am humbled by my time with them.

Virginia's lesson of always "being an original" came back to me so often. She insisted that people do not follow a guru's cause because, at best, they will be second in their field. She insisted on originality, and Esalen cemented that lesson for me. The teachers I experienced were not the guru types.

The Johnson Institute

*"Success is accepting failure, building inspiration
on a daily basis to accept failure yet again and appreciate
the lifetime it took to succeed."*

—Jasmina Siderovski

With both Nurturing Networks and The House in business, these were good years professionally. One day, a reporter from the *Minneapolis Star* called me and asked for an interview. It ended up being two whole pages in the Variety section of the Sunday paper.

The next week, a call came from a board member of a well-known intervention center. He offered me a job at an agency called the Johnson Institute (JI), an intervention center with an international reputation. They asked me, and half of my staff, to form a new department called "Family Care." The other half of my team could keep "The House" and the good work they were doing. I had interned at the Johnson Institute for three months and was familiar with their work. I accepted and also became a member of the five-member management team. That turned out to be a good move.

We split The House staff right down the middle, and half of them went with me to JI. Everyone was happy and a new era began.

The Family Care department was developed, and we began treating family members and facilitating support and therapy groups for spouses, siblings, young adults, and children. Soon the programs became the largest department at the Johnson Institute. It was the early seventies when we began to get requests to bring these programs to treatment centers. I was the person who began this arduous task.

I decided to write a one-week family program for addiction treatment programs. I think we were the first in the nation to do that. We tried out our prototype at Baton Rouge General Hospital in Louisiana and then at St. Mary's Hospital in Minneapolis. While the Minnesota hospitals had boundaries on what they allowed to happen, Baton Rouge was ahead of their time, and we installed the full and complete program I had always dreamed about. It was a major success.

This really built my confidence; I knew we had a five-day program that was significant and helped families in a most amazing way. This was the birth of the five-day family treatment program. The trick was how to get it paid for, and that brought a new challenge. Each treatment center began working on how to slip the family treatment program into their treatment plan. Different treatment programs came up with different plans.

LESSONS LEARNED

When I developed The House programs, there was so much gratitude and happiness that I thought I would be there forever. Getting the call from the Johnson Institute told me that my Higher Power was at work and that it wasn't always going to be up to me to plan my life. This lesson gave me great comfort and increased my faith. It was another gift from the universe.

During my time at the Institute, my travels took me to many places in the world. The JI had a contract with the air force for my family programs, and I visited many air force bases in several countries. I learned this is a much bigger world than I had known about.

Changes at the Johnson Institute

*"Innovation distinguishes between a
leader and a follower."*

—Steve Jobs

Bringing the family programs developed at The House to the Johnson Institute changed the direction and the complexion of the Institute. It was a renowned intervention center with a reputation that touched the whole United States and extended overseas.

The first part of my assignment was to be part of the only female professional interventionist's job and learn the "JI" way of doing an intervention. The second part of my assignment was to be the only female on a male management team. In my months of apprenticeship with her, I was part of hundreds of interventions. It became abundantly clear to me that our interventions were successful because we trained the families so well. Soon I was doing them by myself and was a part of countless successful interventions.

However, when it was over and the intended went to a treatment center, the families were then on their own. The treatment center sometimes offered lectures on what to do when their addict or alcoholic came home, but there was nothing to help the family with what they could or should do for themselves and all the trauma they had gone through. From personal experience, there were all the memories of that time and the feelings about that time did not go away. In recovery for the addict or alcoholic, there were now more reasons for their needs to remain the center of attention in the home and the children were basically ignored.

My mission became to provide care for the rest of the family. I wanted to help spouses find help for themselves and ultimately avoid new addiction in the family in the children. It was a long and tedious battle, but eventually my thoughts and ideas were honored by some of the members of the board of directors who had families of their own and agreed completely. The president of the company was not on board. The board, over his head, gave me a spot on the management team and made me part of the decision-making process for the institute. My role was to be the second woman employed, and then to be on the management team was unheard of. Women had previously been support staff, not leaders.

Lessons Learned

One lesson I learned was that, very often, my role was to be the first of something. Because the alcoholism family disease concept was just beginning at this time, trails hadn't been blazed. It seemed that was my job.

To my knowledge, at that time the first five-day inpatient family treatment program was developed at Baton Rouge General Hospital, Louisiana. If there were others, I don't know about them. This would have been in the early seventies. More than ever, I learned the family needed to have their own treatment programs, not just one tacked on to the alcoholic's treatment program.

Air Force Family Programs

"It doesn't matter whether you are pursuing success
in business, sports, the arts, or life in general.
The bridge between wishing and
accomplishing is discipline."

—Harvey Mackay

The Johnson Institute had many training programs and I became heavily involved in two of them. One was the United States Air Force. Our intervention programs were the heart of JI, and the air force wanted intervention training, and to learn about the concept of alcoholism as a family illness.

The institute had two people who could travel and do the intervention training, but the air force insisted that I be the one who did the family training. That began a year of heavy travel. My challenge was to visit every base in the United States and several in Europe, including Ramstein in Germany, Lakenheath in England, and others. I loved the work!

I named them "my boys in blue." What I noticed was how grateful they were, how punctual they were, and how hungry they were for the information. There was none of the resistance or passive-aggressive behavior that met me in the addiction field in the therapy groups back in the United States. The addiction field was not always welcoming to the family aspects of the disease.

At that time, women did not travel alone. The air force assigned me what they called a "bodyguard" who I traveled with in Europe. (I ran into him again in recent years: when he left the air force and became director of a treatment center.)

Another favorite experience was at Hill Air Force Base in northern Utah. One of the council of twelve, those who direct the Church of the Latter-Day Saints in that state, had attended one of my family workshops in Minnesota.

He invited me and the church, with the support of Hill Air Force Base, contracted with me to write a Sunday night family book and also make a movie about the family illness of addiction. It was a great experience for me and a warm, inviting group of people to work with.

LESSONS LEARNED

Through the air force consultations and workshops, I learned how valuable the military is to all of us. Oftentimes, I would live on base, and mix and mingle with officers, airmen, and their families. Unless involved at some level, I realized we don't often think about the life lived in the military. Many a morning, an alarm clock was not needed as the men were out running with their cadence calls.

Freedom Fest

"Celebration is a human need that we must not,
and cannot, deny. It's richer when many
work and then celebrate together."
—Carita Kent and Jan Stewart

Minneapolis became the hub of chemical dependency addiction treatment in the early seventies. One of the main reasons was that we had a governor who had a major interest in addiction and recovery. He signed a multimillion dollar piece of legislation that helped many treatment programs get a head start.

Another reason is that Minnesota had the largest group of Employee Assistance Programs (EAP) in the nation. The city was home to many headquarters of industry, who recognized the value of treating their employees well.

Another factor was the Johnson Institute intervention-training programs. There was a time when most employee assistance programs expected each employee to go through intervention training. There were so many people doing intervention programs that there were hardly enough programs to get the job done. There were twenty-six inpatient programs and countless outpatient programs in Minnesota at that time.

Freedom Fest was held in Minnesota early in the nineteen seventies. Movie stars George Gobel and Dick Van Dyke, yogi Swami Rama, Virginia Satir, and others were on hand for the program, along with sports stars, musicians, and more.

As some 26,000 people began arriving for a full day's celebration, there was a torrential rainstorm. Water was running everywhere and people were getting soaked. No one cared. You could hear people saying, "After what I have been through, no little rain is going to stop me." Loudspeakers were wrapped in plastic to protect them, and the show went on. When Dick Van Dyke came onstage, his first words were "This is the wettest group of 'drys' I have ever seen." It was a historical meeting of recovery.

LESSONS LEARNED

My takeaway from the Freedom Fest was that all strata of people are in recovery. From Dick Van Dyke to my uncle from Colorado, everyone was celebrating along with treatment professionals, clients, and AA members. All ages from teens to old people, men and women, were represented. It appears that nothing about addiction or alcoholism is discriminating.

Minnesota North Stars

"A team is a group of people with complementary
skills who work together to achieve a goal."
—Bonnie Edelstein

Years ago, the chairman of the board of my company, Onsite, was one of the owners of the Minnesota North Stars NHL hockey team. His best friend was another owner. Both owners had therapists for their families. I was one of them, and a friend of mine, Bob Moran, was the other. The North Stars were doing very badly and hadn't been winning for a couple of years.

The owners asked my friend Bob and me if we would do some work with the team. They wanted to know if we could use what we knew about family system counseling to try and help a sports team. We weren't sure, but agreed to give it a try.

The team nicknamed us the "shrinks." We are both small in stature and up against their well-honed hockey bodies; we did look like we were a bit disadvantaged. We weathered a couple of sessions, concerned we would never be taken seriously.

Then one day while they were practicing on the ice, Bob went down, put on his ice skates, skated out, and asked to skate with them. Little did they know he was an accomplished Canadian skater and had blazing speed; Bob skated circles around them. Our stature rose immediately. Then I asked for time with their wives and girlfriends.

It was all very revealing. We found that older hockey wives were very much like older corporate wives. They were willing to go anywhere and sacrifice their own lives for their husbands' careers. Younger hockey wives and girlfriends wanted more for themselves. They were married or dating much younger men who were making more money than they ever imagined. Conflict brewed between the older and younger women. This conflict translated into "pillow talk," and led to the players bringing conflicts onto the ice.

Our next step was to reconcile the wives' feelings about each other. We encouraged the younger wives to learn from the older ones. They had been managing living with a sports star for some time and had some great tips. We encouraged the older wives to be a little more assertive, like the younger wives, and they liked that new behavior. The women became friends, and the men played better hockey. My friend and I enjoyed some of those new games. Later, they won the Stanley Cup. It was a successful adventure. One of my daughters became a real fan of the North Stars, especially popular star Dino Ciccarelli. She had a couple of dinosaurs as stuffed animal toys in his honor.

The night she turned sixteen, I asked Lou Nanne, general manager of the North Stars, Dino, and a few other players to surprise her at her party. She was thrilled!

LESSONS LEARNED

First, I learned a great deal about hockey, from the effort, the practicing, the physicality of it all, and the fact that professional athletes are basically just people. I also learned they don't think much about their feelings and relationships. The game does come first.

The second lesson was how much fun it was to work with the North Stars. They were funny and loyal to each other. I found myself invested in them, and when one of the players broke his ankle and ended up in the hospital, I went there to take flowers "from the shrink." It was a grand experience.

Olga Worrall, Psychic and Sage

*"The concept of psychic energy is easy for most
people to imagine. After all, it's just one step beyond
intuition—and almost everyone is comfortable
with the idea of intuition."*

—Jayne Ann Krentz

When I was training with Virginia Satir, she invited me to Baltimore to meet Olga Worrall, the mystic with healing hands.

She was a well-known spiritual and psychic healer. Olga and her husband Ambrose were well-known as very spiritual people. After the death of her husband in 1972, she went on to national prominence for bringing healing back to churches. Olga believed in community and usually chose to do her healing in a church setting. Even though she went on to do extensive healing work alone after her husband's death, she still signed my book *Ambrose and Olga Worrall.*

Olga introduced me to another depth of healing. When she prayed over and with me, the heat from her hands was penetrating and touched me deeply. She had the incredible power to mentally, emotionally, and physically heal those with whom she prayed. On one TV show, Johns Hopkins Hospital re-created a cloud chamber. Olga was able to put her hands on the chamber and make it rain. She was also known for being able to make a physical diagnosis simply by being in the room with someone.

Olga shared with Virginia and me her thoughts about the power of "healing at a distance." She believed that using the energy of someone on Earth can produce a physical connection over long distances. Olga felt she could be one of those people. She felt that spiritual healing is similar to electricity; she called it "paraelectricity."

According to Olga, spiritual healing is the channeling of energy into a recipient from the universal field of energy, which is common to all creation and which stems from the universal source of all intelligence and power, called God.

At her invitation, we attended a session in which Kirlian photography was used. This type of photography shows the electrical energy in a living thing. The session we attended was too astonishing for me to describe here. It involved watching a soul leave the body.

My personal experience with Olga occurred when my son was attending school in France. He had fallen ill and needed help. He called me. It was a difficult time because he needed to travel and search for help. We lost contact for a few days in the crisis. In my desperation, I called Olga. She wanted his name, age, location, and symptoms. Olga prayed with me and told me, "Do not worry. He is getting help getting home. When he arrives home, ask him to seek help where he goes to college. They will make the correct diagnosis and he will have surgery and recover. Basically, right now he is spiritually healed."

A short time later, my son arrived looking thin and tired. With encouragement he went to Colorado, (back to his school) where he received a diagnosis, had surgery, and recovered completely. In my call back to her, she said, "All healing comes through wisdom, knowledge, faith, and God."

LESSONS LEARNED

Olga taught me that true spirituality is quite humble. Prior to that, some of it seemed like a mystery, and only a few people could be considered true spirits. She taught me that we are all as spiritual as we want to be. Her humility etched an important lesson in my heart and in my soul. I truly saw and experienced the difference between religion and spirituality.

The Freedom Institute

"He or she is rich or poor according to what they are,
not according to what they have."
—Henry Ward Beecher

There was another institute in New York City that patterned itself after the Johnson Institute of Minneapolis. While the JI mainly did interventions with employee-assistance programs in corporations and offered one-week training schools, the focus was different in New York. Many of the interventions were for very high-profile people. It was and continues to be a wonderful program, and I was proud to be part of its beginning, serving as a consultant in the early days to help put it all together.

I had done five-day training sessions for Mona Mansell, the owner and president of the Freedom Institute. She had also selected me to be an advisor to her board of directors. This meant going to New York every three months for board meetings. Usually, I would stay a week and also train counselors in a live-in training event held in Manhasset, New York.

What I liked best about my New York trips was that I often was able to take my youngest daughter along. She loved New York and made a very good friend that is still in her life today. It gave us some important time together.

The friend that invited me to her agency also invited me to stay in her home on Park Avenue. Each time I arrived in a cab on Park Avenue for a board meeting at a major New York City bank, I realized what a long way I'd come from Comfrey, Minnesota.

LESSONS LEARNED

I discovered that there is a common thread shared by people around addiction. Growing up in a small town in Minnesota was very different from Manhattan. Yet illness is the same in both settings, whether measles or addiction. The family-disease concept helped people in both places and the training for counselors was the same.

Struggles Writing My First Book

"God doesn't give you the people you want.
He gives you the people you need. To help you, hurt you,
to leave you, to love you, to respect you, and to make
you into the person you were meant to be."

—Anonymous

Virginia Satir had introduced me to a psychiatrist in California who specialized in programs for children who had been sexually abused. I worked with him on and off for about three months and learned a great deal about incest, other sexual abuse, and the legal system and its response (and failure to respond) to domestic and sexual abuse cases. He was also a publisher who was very interested in my work. He invited me to submit a manuscript about my work with families dealing with addiction.

While writing my book and working at the Johnson Institute (JI), I discovered that the president of the institute was not in favor of women professionals. This was before the women's movement and before sexism was spoken about. Yet I was a victim of it. Until I was hired, women at the JI could only be secretaries or bookkeepers; they were not allowed in management or decision-making positions. I was the first. Since I was hired by the board and not by the president, there were some who were concerned that I might be discriminated against. Innocent me . . . I didn't catch on.

It was a challenging time. As my family programs began to outshine the intervention programs, the situation only became harder. When I started writing my first book, the president came to me and said I couldn't publish without his approval. In my innocence, I believed him. This resulted in a year of rewriting and rewriting and pure exhaustion trying to get his approval. I had manuscripts of this book in every cupboard.

One day I was doing a lecture in one of my training programs and I heard myself telling people that often the time comes when people have to cut loose from some "holding back" experience and simply go on. My personal holding-back experience was an employer who didn't approve of women in general or employees that might be a bit different from him, and who was not supportive of my work.

I finished my lecture and went back to work and resigned from my position. I was a single parent, making more money than I had ever made, and felt secure. It didn't matter. My heart was breaking, my soul was devastated, and I needed to act. I quit with two weeks' notice. The company was so threatened by me that they didn't have me finish the two weeks.

As the institute started working on my exit paperwork, they discovered that many of the training contracts they held were on the condition that I would be the one who delivered the training. To not break the contracts, they had to allow me a few months of consulting work with them at the going market rate. They had been making a great deal of money on my work; these consulting fees added up to more than I had been making in salary. This gave me a head start.

Best of all, the book, *Another Chance: Hope and Health for the Alcoholic Family*, was published in 1981. It became a best seller and, thirty-five years later, it's considered a classic in treatment programs, colleges, mental health centers, etc. Royalties are still coming in. The JI tried to take credit for my roles. Family Hero, Scapegoat, Lost Child, and Mascot because I worked there while I was writing. I fought back and won.

LESSONS LEARNED

I learned to stand up for myself. This was the event that convinced me that my work was good, very good, and that it was time I "made some noise" by fighting for the publishing rights. Eventually I hired an attorney. This required more money than I had at the time, so I borrowed funds to win back my rights. That book became the cornerstone of my career and was worth every penny I spent on it.

"No boundary or barrier surrounds the heart of a person who loves self and others."

—*Shannon L. Alder*

Leaving the Johnson Institute

*"We all want progress, but if you're on the wrong road,
progress means doing an about-turn and walking back to the
right road; in that case, the man who turns back
soonest is the most progressive."*

—C. S. Lewis

It was the right decision to leave the institute, but it was very frightening. My whole family depended on my salary, and all of my children were in college.

Through a friend who gave me a small office in his treatment center, I continued fulfilling the contracts from the institute that specified that the staff member doing the workshops would be me. There was about a year's worth of work already booked.

Even though money was very tight, I hired a film company to come in and record my lecture on the family illness on 16 millimeter film. Workshop participants and trainers had been telling me they would like to have this information for their programs. The film began to sell immediately. Between the book, *Another Chance,* and the film, *The Family Trap,* it was my first experience with so-called passive income; work one time and experience ongoing income in royalties. Thirty-plus years later, the movie and book continue to sell. There has never been a year without income from just those two products, plus the information has stood the test of time and helped many individuals, families, and programs.

During this time I moved on from the hurt and sadness about leaving JI. It had truly became my identity for a time. Not only had I interned there, but also become an interventionist, with some 500 interventions—most of them successful. I had created my own type of intervention with the whole family committing to treatment. Often, the family went to treatment before the addict did. This made the addict's intervention so much easier and more likely to be successful. Because my interventions were unique, my training sessions were always full.

Leaving the institute was the path I needed to take. I had to forgive and move on with a clear and clean heart. Faith is the hope we hang on to when our life is falling apart.

LESSONS LEARNED

Each time something like this happened, I learned that life is a journey and that we have many destinations. I learned that it wasn't so frightening anymore to take chances and move on.

I remembered Virginia telling me earlier, "You are not turning your back; you are just going in a new direction." She assured me that, as my comings and goings became more frequent, they would become less frightening.

Don and I Divorce

*"I was so devastated by my second divorce that
I had a nervous breakdown."*

—Jane Fonda

By the time the end came at the Johnson Institute, the book was published, and my movie filmed, it was clear that my model of the alcoholic family had real value.

However, home was not happy. Don and I were going in different directions and wanted very different lifestyles. My path was developing programs for alcoholic families and getting people to those programs. Don really wanted a nine-to-five job with plenty of time for socializing, reading, and down time. My work included many nights and weekends. Our lifestyles just didn't work together. We supported each other's work and agreed on many things philosophically and pragmatically, yet we wanted different futures.

Don went to Esalen with me and we decided to be honest about our relationship. Our mutual realization was that we should have been each other's counselors instead of spouses. We had helped each other heal our childhoods and first commitments. At this time we chose to separate and thank each other for the role we played in each other's lives. It was a healing twelve years together.

I will always be grateful to him for how good he was to and for my children. Our separation and eventual divorce was right for both of us. He has gone on and found a person to share his lifestyle, and eventually I found my soul mate. We are happy for each other.

LESSONS LEARNED

I learned much from Don; he had such an easy way about him. Until I met him, my life was so serious and so responsible. He made me laugh and gave me a break from my own steadfastness.

Learning to play and take some time for myself was new to me; even taking our pleasure trip to Hawaii was a new thing. For the first time, my family and I learned to enjoy ourselves, including camping.

He inspired me to take in foreign exchange students. Don had traveled more extensively, and he brought different cultures to my awareness. He was a gentle man and it felt safe to be married to him. That was also new for me.

Esalen taught Don and me that we could be better friends than spouses, and other very important lessons. It was where we decided to move on from our marriage together.

Chapter Five

ONSITE BEGINS

Angels Appear

*"When someone lets us know they are there for us
and that they want to help us 'one more time,' it feels like we
are coming out of a fog. For the moment, we know we
will survive and someone will help us do so."*

—Unknown

Once again, the same two angels that invited me to the Johnson Institute approached me. The couple—Irene and Wheelock Whitney—had total faith in me and my work. They told me they could put together a small group of investors and support me in developing a company to train corporations and helping professionals. Instead of being only an intervention company, they wanted me to develop a new company (Onsite) that would identify, intervene, and also treat the needs of the whole family. The concept of family treatment became a field of its own.

They rented a four-room office in downtown Minneapolis and named me president of this new company. We also hired an executive director and a secretary. We named this company "The Center for the Development of Human Potential." It was a great company and we were instantly full of requests for training seminars. We did a great deal of work with corporations who found my family model very helpful to their companies and board of directors. My travels took me to corporations around the United States.

With the phones ringing off the hook, the name "The Center for the Development of Human Potential" became too difficult for answering phones. We legally changed our official name to "Onsite Training and Consulting." It was a winner—easy to say and easy to remember. We promised to deliver our training and consulting as "Onsite."

Soon we had contracts with Northwest Airlines, Burlington Northern Railroad, Bache & Company investment firm, Dain Bosworth investment firm, Cargill, Inc., the Mormon church organization in Utah, countless military bases, colleges, universities, mental health centers, and, of course, addiction programs and treatment centers everywhere.

We started work in 1978 and worked diligently until 1981, when I left and moved to Texas to accept a new position. Onsite was really me; when I left, it closed its doors and became dormant in terms of training. My work there included producing another film, called *Another Chance*, which remained in Minnesota with Onsite, which owned this very expensive film.

I had gathered thirty people together and looked for one special person to attempt to do a fourteen-hour reconstruction marathon just like the one Virginia did with me. Our movie would have props and experiential sculptures, and, in later reconstructions, music.

Mary Lee Zawadski, a well-known trainer and therapist, was asked to be the star. She agreed and was magnificent. The film turned out to be both an intervention and training film, and was shown for years at conferences and addiction and mental health centers. It is still available on DVD. It was the first live experiential training event. Virginia's reconstruction film with me was also live, but not as experiential.

Even in those years, it was a very expensive film to make; that cost becomes an important factor later in my story. My company continued to distribute this film, but all training programs and consulting stopped when I left. It was very hard for me to leave the film behind, but it was owned by Onsite, and I had left Onsite. Years later, I bought back the company and the film.

LESSONS LEARNED

The angels brought more learning about having faith and letting the universe and God provide the opportunities. What a thrill to become president of a company that wants to do the work that has become my passion. My confidence and courage had grown enough that I made the decision to try a new program. The reconstruction became a very important event and process. Lesson learned: follow your heart and the rest will be given to you.

Texas Invitation

"There are minor regrets and major regrets.
Never will I underestimate the power of a decision.
You cannot beat yourself up forever. You just get wiser."

—Sharon Wegscheider-Cruse

There was a beautiful, intelligent, and wealthy woman I knew in Austin, Texas. She had attended many of my programs and offered me several consulting roles that had gone very well. When she heard I was leaving the Johnson Institute, and learned of my role at the Freedom Institute in New York, she offered me an important position in a treatment and training center she was developing in Austin, Texas. Accepting would mean moving there.

That was one of my hardest decisions ever. Minnesota had been my home for more than forty years. Moving meant leaving so many things dear to me. The Midwest had always been my home.

All of my children were in college, but it still felt as if I was leaving them. Her offer was three times what I had ever earned. There was revenue from Nurturing Networks, now run by my daughters, which covered their living expenses and their college. But the Austin money would be a lifesaver.

I will never know if this was the right decision, but I moved to Austin with lots of ambivalent feelings. The deciding factor was having more income when my family and I needed it. The next story flows out of this ambivalence.

LESSON LEARNED

Not all lessons and gifts come without strings attached. The Texas invitation was so right in so many ways. Yet perhaps I left Minnesota too soon. All of my children were in college and it felt safe to follow this work. Yet, if it were to be done again, I might not do it. My lesson was to take plenty of time and consider all consequences.

Red Rose

*"I had absolutely nothing to back me up
except a deeply rooted resolution and belief. My belief
was formed by life and experience and
a deep feeling within me."*

—Sharon Wegscheider-Cruse

Moving to Austin, Texas brought up huge fear about leaving my home state and all my life experience up until then behind. What would happen with my two girls in college in Minnesota, and my son, who was studying out of state in Colorado? Was this really where God was directing me? Would anyone ever know me professionally outside of Minnesota?

With deep fear and apprehension, I started out in my little car for the long ride to Austin. It was January, so there was concern about snow and road conditions. The first day was a bit exciting and the roads were good. The second day, however, it snowed, and the feeling of loss began to hit me hard. I started to cry. Doubts were haunting me. I drove through snow and ice, crying quietly all the way.

About three o'clock in the afternoon, I stopped at a truck stop to have a snack. There was a stack of magazines on a table in front. Picking up one and ordering coffee, I thumbed through the magazine. Then I saw this headline on the cover: "Sharon Wegscheider Helps Addictive Families Recover, page 37." Going to that page, I learned that someone I didn't know had written an article about a lecture I had delivered at a college. My takeaway was that maybe my professional life wouldn't disappear just because of my move.

When the waitress appeared, the first thing she said was, "Hi, you must be the Red Rose." Puzzled, I asked what that meant. She said, "All day truck drivers have been coming in and talking about a lone lady in a Chevy driving out of Minneapolis and headed south on icy roads. She has a red hat, red boots, and red gloves. They named you "The Red Rose." They have been following you and looking after you." More tears flowed as the feeling that I was being watched over and cared for swept through me.

Back in the car, driving on slippery roads, it felt that I was doing the right thing, that I would not be forgotten, and that my God was there for me.

LESSONS LEARNED

My protection was very strong and my universal love will never leave me, even when I doubt myself. My faith is strong. The lesson I learned that I was never really alone, and this last story about the Red Rose convinced me. I felt I had made the right decision.

Conferences, Keynotes, and Workshops

"Some people come into our lives and quickly go.
Some stay a while, leave footprints, and
we are never, ever the same."

—Flavia Weedn

What can I say? Public speaking is an honor and a humbling experience. From a shy little girl, through high school oratory, to a national public speaker, it has become one of my loves. Give me a microphone and I am in my element.

Looking out into the eyes of an audience remains a high for me. It feels like they send energy that goes deep inside and somehow connects us all together. There is always a story to tell, information to share, and a connection to be made.

Over thirty years, there have been hundreds and hundreds of these experiences, and each one remains a treasure. The family illness of addiction, intervention, relationships, sexuality, corporate issues, loss and grief, wellness, spirituality—the list of topics goes on and on. I have loved all the presentations, even the ones that threatened to go sideways.

One time, at Harvard, in a conference room in the middle of a lecture, I saw this man get up and go outside at the back of the room. Then he started bringing flowers in and putting them around the podium. It was a little unnerving, but there were about 200 people in the room so I just kept going. Eventually, he brought candles and lit them. I kept speaking but was getting very uncomfortable. I signaled for my host to come to the podium, where I gave him a note, while continuing to speak, to remove this man. Quietly, without anyone skipping a beat, he was escorted out of my workshop and security took over.

Another time in Pennsylvania, after a presentation about addictive families, several people crowded around me, wanting more information. The crowd became demanding, and someone ripped the sleeve off my blouse. That became the last time I ever left the podium and walked through the crowd alone.

Another time in Colorado Springs, a waiter kept knocking on my hotel room late at night trying to deliver food I had not ordered. Several times, I refused to answer his knock on my door and eventually demanded that the hotel send up security. Security stayed outside my door for the rest of the evening. Next day, I found out a woman had been murdered in that room two weeks before.

Not all unexpected experiences were negative. My favorite memory was of Clearwater Beach, delivering a workshop on my birthday. As I finished my talk, I saw two of my favorite sages, Peter Vegso and Gary Seidler, come walking down the aisle with a giant birthday cake and fifty red roses, while leading the audience of a few hundred people in singing "Happy Birthday" to me.

It was a major thrill for me to be the keynote speaker for the first National Conference on Children of Alcoholics, the first Codependency Conference, and the first Conference on the Family Illness. These were major milestones in the field, and to be a major part of them filled me with joy.

The thousands of miles in airplanes, the hundreds of hotel stays, and the countless restaurant meals can't compare with the satisfaction and joy of meeting people of all ages and all walks of life and connecting eye-to-eye. That has been a true blessing.

LESSONS LEARNED

What I learned from countless conferences, lectures, and workshops was how to travel and create a network. There have been hotel/motel experiences; single-engine, one-pilot planes to DC10's; cars and private town cars. The variety of restaurants and foods I encountered expanded my interest in dining. My travels have enriched my life in so many ways; I feel richly blessed. I have spoken in every state, parts of Europe, Canada, Mexico, Australia, and New Zealand.

Texas Surprise

"There are two ways to get ahead.
Agree with the boss, or be the boss.
Which do you prefer?"

—Old Saying

After about nine months, the Texas culture was beginning to feel manageable. It was like no other job I had experienced. My boss was an amazing woman to work with. She believed in my work, trusted my work ethic, and knew I could adapt and meet her needs.

First of all, while I had an office of my own and a full-time secretary, she understood that my work was partly therapy, partly intuitive, many parts healing, and some parts drama. She gave me full support and the freedom to work in nontraditional ways. If I felt inspired in my pajamas at home, she urged me to work from home. If I did a late-night psychodrama, she insisted I stay home and rest the next day. She trusted my outcomes, not the standard way of doing things. We accomplished great things together.

It would not be unusual for her to tell me to take a day off when she had something big she wanted me to do. Once she told me to go shopping and buy a ball gown, price no object, because I needed to look good. I did. She then announced that she had put together an evening of movers and shakers from the Austin area. She asked me to show up and be prepared to "do my thing," which was a classy presentation on the family illness and secrets in painful families. She trusted me and I trusted her. I felt like a princess in a designer ball gown—not like a lecturer.

It was a typical gathering of all of the city's elite in gowns and tuxedos. It was a lovely evening and dinner. During dessert, champagne was served with an announcement of a special treat. The waiters brought a large blackboard onto the stage, and it was announced that I was going to do a forty-five minute presentation that would knock their socks off. I went up to the stage, ball gown and all, and prepared to "do my thing." It ended in a rousing round of applause. Many had never heard a presentation from someone in an elegant gown, draped in jewelry with her hair all done up. The upshot was that this major fund-raising night exceeded all expectations.

Two days later, I was back in a conservative suit to appear before the National Association of Insurance Commissioners to plead the case for insurance coverage for addiction treatment. This was an intense three-day examination, interview, and questioning by top-notch lawyers. We won that case as well. I still have the letter telling us what a wonderful job we did. Life in Texas built my confidence and we made many plans.

LESSONS LEARNED

From this benefactor and Texas I learned that there are many ways to do the same thing; that money was power; and that sometimes you follow the adage, "When in Rome, do as the Romans do." All of my events in this state were big, different, and powerful. It was a great learning experience.

I discovered the River Walk in San Antonio, where I would consistently take my group leaders after a program. I learned to live in a country club area and felt great independence.

Meeting Joe Cruse

*"It's like a clear note of music meeting
with another clear note and finding a harmony.
Two journeys come together at a moment of time and
that harmony makes music. Add recovery and
a spiritual power and that becomes
'the only dance there is' for both of you."*
—Sharon Wegscheider-Cruse

During the years of speaking, doing workshops, and consulting, many of the people on the national circuit would know about each other but not have met. I had known Claudia Black through her writing and in general, but it was years before we met.

Another person I was aware of was Joseph Cruse, MD. We had been introduced years earlier when he came to a training school where I was teaching. Someone brought him up to the podium. He said he always remembered that meeting; I don't remember it at all. However, I knew the name because he was on the board of directors for the National Council on Alcoholism.

While speaking at another conference in Georgia, once again he introduced himself. At the International Doctors in Alcoholics Anonymous (IDAA) conference, we shared some time together and began dating. Eventually, he chose to come to Texas to go through one of my five-day family schools.

One of my daughters attended that program, and I was thrilled to have her there. It was a long and successful week and we finished up by sharing what the week had been like for each participant. When it came to Joe's turn, he said how he enjoyed the week, but he had one question for me: "Would you marry me?" It was a very public proposal. Everyone was a bit stunned, including me. I said yes—and the rest is history.

Up to this time, my career had been busy, amazing, full, and satisfying. I decided to retire, move to California, and marry Joe. Soon, at age forty-five, I quit my job and retired from public life.

LESSONS LEARNED

When you meet your soul mate, you will know it. From almost our first date, I knew we were meant to be together. There was much to do for that to happen, but I learned that if something is meant to be, one will find a way.

Restless in Palm Springs

*"Promise me you will always remember
you are braver than you believe, and stronger than
you seem and smarter than you think."*

—Christopher Robin to Pooh

Moving to Palm Springs/Palm Desert, California was not a good move for me. We had a very fractured lifestyle. Joe was working long hours as founding medical director of the Betty Ford Center, there was a weekend Awareness Hour, a well-attended weekly event to help people become aware of addiction, and he had many social obligations such as dinners and rounds of golf. It felt like we had very little time together.

Prior to this, my time had been filled with groups, connection with others, and some down time. It felt as though I no longer had an identity or privacy. I tried very hard to do the Palm Springs wife thing, but my soul was restless and my mind was stuck.

What had been my mission, my interest, and my life seemed to no longer exist. The days were long. I had never been a shopping or lunching person or had so much time to myself. It was all very boring.

So we decided that I would go back to work. I had kept a private secretary because when I retired there was a year of loose ends to handle. She moved to Palm Springs with me when I moved there.

What I decided to do was to try to buy the company that I had been president of and own it. This company was still known as Onsite Training and Consulting, and it lay dormant in Minnesota except for continuing to sell my film, *Another Chance*. Inside I knew that my years of private practice, except for facilitating reconstructions, were over; my passion was to teach, train, and consult.

I got a bit of a shock on the price when inquiring about buying Onsite. The price was set high to pay off the debt of making the film. No way did I have access to that much money. However, I was earning income from royalties and properties.

It seemed to me that income and assets would qualify me to get a loan of some kind, either personal or business. My eyes were forever opened. This was the early 1980's and interest rates were sky high. Each bank had a different reason for turning me down, but one banker was quite honest. I was a woman, and banks at that time were not giving loans to women who wanted to start businesses.

A bit taken aback, and very much infuriated by such complete rejection, it was clear that drastic measures would be required. There was a very wealthy man who had been through my programs and impressed by their content and unique group leader structure. He agreed to loan me the funds I needed in exchange for 10 percent ownership of the company. This was not the way I wanted to buy Onsite, but there was really no other way. It was a verbal agreement that he would give me the stock back when I paid back the loan. I trusted him.

It took two years and the entire loan was paid back. By then, Onsite was doing very well and he decided he wanted to keep his ownership. He would not honor our agreement. It took almost two years of negotiating with him before he finally gave me his 10 percent with an additional payoff. Onsite was now mine and mine alone.

LESSONS LEARNED

The time in Palm Springs taught me an important lesson about lifestyle. Mine was simpler, more informal, and more rustic than that of the beautiful California oasis. Minnesota and Texas were much more my style, which includes following my passion and working.

The life of leisure and golf held no interest for me. It seemed too old and too static. Work was a good fit for me; it was too soon to retire.

Back in the Business of Onsite

"The soul is restless and will keep us restless
until we are fulfilled."
—Anthony Padavano

Now that I was back in business, I met a banker who respected my work and saw the value of it. As soon as I had enough money from running Onsite programs, I put a down payment on a condo that became the Onsite office. Work became my focus and I worked at making peace with living in the Palm Springs/Palm Desert.

My days were filled with Onsite programs and our evenings with many social obligations. Joe's job was demanding, five days a week that often included nights. Every Friday night we also had dinner as part of Joe's volunteer work, and he also worked Saturdays until about 2:00 PM.

Our time was rarely our own. Joe was becoming more and more interested in the family aspects of Onsite and enjoyed the many group leaders who came to California to work in my programs. We seemed to be busy with obligations day and night.

At the same time, we had a wonderful sage that we worked with trying to reconcile our fairly fractured lifestyles. We wanted someone who didn't know either of us professionally. We found him in Palo Alto, California. He had never heard of either of us. *Perfect.* We would go to Palo Alto when we had time, and he would work with us.

His name was John. We would save up issues and differences in our "John" file and then make a trip. If we could arrange enough time, we would rent a room in the airline's private lounge and maybe do six or seven hours at a stretch. Joe and I learned that Palm Springs/Palm Desert was not a good place for the kind of work we both wanted to do.

That year, a professional friend of Joe's invited us to South Dakota to spend Easter with him and his wife. Not having been to the Black Hills before, we both thought it would be a good break. That Easter morning brought us to Mount Rushmore at daybreak for a sunrise service. It was beautiful, peaceful, and inspiring. We looked at each other and said, "This is it." We made a decision that we were going to live in the Black Hills of South Dakota, somewhere near Rapid City.

People ask us if it was a culture shock. We say yes, it was the best shock we could have had. We started out in Sioux Falls and Onsite moved with me. Joe started out in Sioux Falls with the River Park Treatment Programs (while also working in Pennsylvania in connection with the Caron Foundation). He was gone a great deal and kept an apartment in Pennsylvania. Now that Onsite was mine along with Nurturing Networks, everything was expanding and growing. It didn't take long before it was clear that I needed more programs to meet the needs of people coming to Onsite programs.

At that point, I made an important decision. I wanted to add a treatment program, and who better to do that than Joe? I made him a job offer. It would mean changes for both of us. I'd have to purchase an office building and a treatment space. We both did a great deal of soul searching. Our work had always been quite separate and quite different from each other's. Would it work for us to actually work together with me as president of the company and Joe as an employee? We each made separate decisions, and we decided it was what each of us wanted.

LESSONS LEARNED

Yes, it was my work that brought me great joy. Joe was busy at the Betty Ford Center and I was back at Onsite; this was good for both of us. Unfortunately, it lasted only a short time as we both grew restless in Palm Springs. We both wanted something more. The lesson learned is that we needed a third-party consultant. The big lesson learned was that we wanted a simpler and more grounded lifestyle; that's why we landed in the beautiful Black Hills of South Dakota. Many lessons learned in a short time together.

A Home in the Black Hills

*"Coming back is the thing that enables you to see
how all the dots in your life are connected, how one decision leads
you to another, how one twist of fate, good or bad, brings you
to a door that later takes you to another door, which, aided by several
detours—long hallways and unforeseen stairwells—
eventually puts you in the place you are now."*

—Ann Patchett

Little did I know when I left Texas that I would move homes thirteen more times. If I had had stock in the Mayflower Moving Company, moving so much might have been a profitable venture. However, each culture change was enriching and offered another view of life. This big move was to South Dakota.

We began the re-establishment of Onsite in Sioux Falls. Joe was still working at that time for a treatment program in that state and also working with the Caron Foundation in Pennsylvania. My role was to work with my former company, Nurturing Networks. I took it over from my family, who had kept it running in Minnesota. Our career adventures were quite different from each other.

Onsite's first new home was my South Dakota basement. My staff had their own entrance and we flourished. But it became clear early on that we needed more space. We had heard about an office building for sale in Rapid City.

We had loved the Black Hills area and were drawn to it. It was there we wanted to work and live. We made a trip there, and I looked at office buildings and Joe looked for a home. We each found what we wanted almost immediately. Much divine intervention here, I do believe.

I found a lawyer's office building for sale. It had three floors, an executive meeting room, four offices, two bathrooms, and what could be three group rooms. It was perfect. I remember meeting with the seller, a friend today, and feeling the good energy of what had been in the building. I had the money for a down payment and a loan was much easier to get at that time and place.

Joe found three places, but saved the best for last as he knew I would love it. It was a log home about four miles from town. It was big enough to house four group leaders when they came to town to work.

The log home was situated on seventeen very private acres. Privacy was becoming very important to me. By then I had been a guest on Phil Donahue, Larry King, and twice on Oprah's show, plus countless local TV and radio shows. My books were reaching people throughout the United States, Australia, New Zealand, Mexico, and Canada. It became important at that time to get unlisted, unpublished phone numbers and protect some private time.

This house was going to be perfect. The office was going to be perfect. All we needed was the perfect place for our residential programs.

LESSONS LEARNED

To be back to a simple lifestyle felt so right. Lesson learned was to find where you fit and go there. Fish belong in water, deer belong in the woods, and I belong with ordinary and simple people. I was home again.

A Place for Our Programs

"The world needs dreamers and the world needs doers.
But above all, the world needs dreamers who do."

—Sarah Ban Breathnach

The final piece of the puzzle—a place to hold our residential programs—took a bit longer to fall in place, but fit perfectly when it did.

When we first moved to Rapid City we rented space in a large convent and spiritual center for our programs. It was called St. Martin's Academy. It had stopped being a school when funds were tight and had become a motherhouse for Benedictine nuns. There were 120 nuns in permanent residence. However, there were extra empty rooms and a commercial kitchen. The nuns would contract with us for meals, and there was a wonderful nun who was in charge of leasing the extra space.

My major concern was that my programs could get loud. When people were working with repressed emotions, there could be screaming, swearing, and other strange sounds. The sister in charge needed to know what she was getting herself into, so we showed her my film *Another Chance*. She watched it, reflected on it, and said, "That is an important work. I will tell the nuns to put bananas in their ears"—and proceeded to sign the contract.

We were there a couple of years, but we had many issues with the kitchen and the food. It was about the time that eating disorders were coming to the fore and our guests were complaining. Despite many attempts to work with the kitchen, the frustration grew. One day, in a negotiation, the sister in charge of the kitchen simply said to me, "You are done. You need to leave by Friday." That was devastating: we had twenty-five people coming in on Saturday for eight days, from all around the country. We scurried to find hotel rooms and a lecture room, but Rapid City is a tourist town, and this was high season.

We were about to cancel the program and reimburse everyone's payment, and their airfares as well, when a place called the Imperial Inn said they had an empty room below their country-western bar and open motel rooms. We jumped at the chance and the program opened Saturday night. As a former dance hall, there were beer signs and cigarette signs all over the walls. During our opening announcements, there was a thumping upstairs as the country line dancing began. It was a rough time. However, all our staff and guests were accepting and gracious. We were forced to stay there until we found an alternative. While there, all of our musical equipment was stolen.

Finally, a couple who owned the Golden Nugget, a wonderful country motel just six miles from Mount Rushmore, agreed to add a commercial kitchen and lecture room. It had twenty-six bedrooms. Four could be group rooms and twenty to forty guests could have bedrooms. It was perfect.

Signing the loan to remodel the Golden Nugget was the biggest financial risk I had ever taken, and it came very soon after buying Onsite. Yet it was divinely inspired and there was no doubt in my mind that it would work. We were about to embark on many golden years in the Black Hills of South Dakota.

LESSON LEARNED

Big lesson learned. Onsite is about healing and learning to live grounded in mind, body, and spirit. It was not going to work in just any setting. An office building had not worked, a convent came close, but not close enough, and certainly a country western bar wasn't going to work. It was time for Onsite to find and develop its own simple healing center in nature's best—the healing and sacred ground of the Black Hills of South Dakota.

Crestwood

"The ache for home lives in all of us, the safe place where
we can go as we are and not be questioned."
—Maya Angelou

Our home was named Crestwood, displayed on a large wooden sign over the driveway. Many people told us that they felt their breathing and heartbeat change as they drove under that sign. Their breathing relaxed while the heart rate rose in joy-filled expectation.

Crestwood was our home while we did our Onsite programs in the Black Hills. Over thirteen years we created a family of professionals. As I traveled around the United States doing professional workshops, some of the best therapists crossed my path: psychologists, social workers, psychiatrists, and psychotherapists. Some excelled in treating addiction, some specialized in eating disorders. There was so much for me to learn from them. And they came to me to experience the combination of psychodrama, music, Gestalt, drama, spirituality, and addiction work that was my way of doing therapy.

In those days, although I had education and abundant training, I didn't see myself as a counselor per se, but more of a natural spiritual healer. Many therapists and I struck an agreement. They would bring their skills to my programs and, at the same time, experience how I worked with clients. This developed into a model that continues at Onsite to this day.

The group leaders formed a family of their own; in many ways, Crestwood became their working family home. It had five bedrooms and bathrooms. Most rooms had two beds, and each treatment team consisted of four or five group leaders. They lived with us for the eight nights they came to the Black Hills. We had a group leader car, and they drove the twenty-two miles to and from work each day.

At night the group leaders would come back to Crestwood and spend some time reviewing each day in the large indoor hot-tub room, surrounded by windows. An occasional deer would peek through the windows. Early morning we met in the angel room, meditated, and offered up our daily work to whatever universal energy, God, Higher Power, or nature was important to each, and then we headed to Onsite.

Miracles took place in the family network of professionals that worked together, and they carried these miracles right into the group rooms each day. What an honor it was to work and live with these sixty-three professionals throughout my career. It has given me brothers and sisters all over the country and makes me feel humbled.

Lessons Learned

Lessons learned at Crestwood were too numerous to count. They included connection, beauty, safety, excitement, meditation, family, weddings, games, music, and miracles.

We loved living in the great outdoors. There were wild turkeys in the backyard, and we had goats (Snap, Crackle, and Pop) and horses (Angel and Star), and many deer.

My family continued to be a primary part of my life, visiting often. Our times together were special with room for everyone. Having my daughter, son-in-law, and two grandsons next door for a while made me very happy.

A lesson I still had to learn was to "let go." The lesson to let them all live their own lives is one that I learned much later.

Chapter Six

GOLDEN YEARS
OF ONSITE

Blessings

*"'Thank you' is the best prayer that anyone could say.
I say that one a lot. Thank you expresses extreme
gratitude, humility, understanding."*

—Alice Walker

Onsite rarely had to advertise. People went home and shared their experience with our programs, and more people came. Soon we were a "go to" for therapists around the country. We had programs for individuals, couples, and families. My dream had come true. Sometimes we advertised with U.S. Journal Training's magazine.

Health Communications invited me to speak at their conferences and we took a booth with them. We had fun with the visitors; that was our form of advertising. National media appearances also helped. I remember the first time Oprah Winfrey's producer called and invited me on the show. My response was, "Who is Oprah?" They explained and assured me that she was going to become a household name. Visibility was high and the Onsite programs flourished.

Writing was also a big part of my life at this time. Eventually, I published eighteen books with two publishers, Health Communications, Inc., and Science and Behavior Books, Inc. Several became bestsellers and today they have been published in thirteen languages. It was also a time of making films, two of which are still selling today.

These years were blessings. I also knew who my boss was; every person who was part of a program or an audience enriched my spiritual life. The whole process felt like a spiritual gift. At that time, nearly 40,000 people had gone through our programs, and since the time I left, thousands more have continued. Onsite had two other owners and the program is thriving today.

One day, it simply happened. I knew I was done. Somewhere toward the end of my Onsite career, I thought of the saying by Erma Bombeck, "When I stand before God at the end of my life, I would hope that I would have not a single bit of talent left and could say, 'I used everything you gave me.'" I knew I would probably never be done producing and creating, but I knew my Onsite time was done.

What to do next was a big challenge, with a couple of false starts. Our first choice to follow us at Onsite betrayed me while I was on a trip to Australia. Our second choice discovered it was simply too much for her. Finally, in the hands of my Higher Power, I dreamed of a couple, Ted Klontz and Margie Zugich, that I knew could do it. I called and they accepted. Onsite went to new owners. It felt like seeing your child grow up and move away or get married. It was a huge loss. I was happy and sad at the same time.

Since I was so identified with Onsite, it was clear that they needed their own identity. So they worked at Onsite, and became known in their own way and later, silently, I just slipped away. They did a wonderful job with Onsite and eventually took the programs to Tennessee, continuing to steward the programs until they sold the company to Miles Adcox, the current owner. Onsite continues to flourish with an owner who feels to me like a spiritual grandson.

LESSONS LEARNED

I could fill a whole book with the lessons I learned from Onsite. I do believe the stars were aligned: the setting, Crestwood, lots of creativity, working with the finest group leaders in the world, strong relationships with Health Communications and Science and Behavior, and the thousands who came to the programs. My seventeen years between 1978 and 1995 were golden. Then to have Ted Klontz and Margie Zugich take over and keep the miracles going until Miles Adcox took the reins. My lesson is that God does provide and to "trust the process."

Reconstructions

"You don't choose your family. They are God's
gift to you, as you are to them."
—Desmond Tutu

Virginia Satir had done the reconstruction process with me, and it had been transforming. Traveling with her and working with her convinced me the process was the single most life-changing event one can have.

Using her basic style and adding new parts to the process became the basis of my programs. My early efforts dated back to the Johnson Institute. By the time the Rapid City reconstructions took place, the model had many new elements.

We had a prop room complete with dolls, clothes, cardboard cut-outs, costumes, wigs, and anything one would have on hand for a drama or movie. Each reconstruction was a major production.

Each "star," or subject, of the reconstruction, would work with me for many months to prepare. I prepared a workbook they would fill out with all the information they had going back as far as they could in their history, coming up to and through their present, and planning after care for their future.

In a therapeutic way we would walk through the star's entire life using this information and whatever psychic energy came to me using the audience, usually about forty people, as role players of their family. It was a combination of Gestalt, psychodrama, history, education, and drama.

During my career, I did about 125 reconstructions and each star I worked with was a treasure to me.

Once we finished the star's process, each attendee would be ready to work on their histories as well. I would have group therapists, with ten in each group, do a day of therapy for an individual group. It was a powerful way to do therapy. Many of my group leaders chose to work in the reconstruction program. One special leader did thirty-two of these one-week programs during her career.

There will always be gratitude in my heart for the early gift that Virginia Satir gave me, and to my Higher Power for the inspiration to create the experiential version.

LESSONS LEARNED

It is in our present strength and power that we find the courage to look into our past and heal. Only then can we go forward with empowerment and clarity. We stand on the shoulders of those who go before us, and I stand on the shoulders of Virginia Satir.

Nicotine Addiction

*"Addiction isn't about substance—you aren't addicted
to the substance, you are addicted to the alteration
of mood the substance brings."*

—Susan Cheever

During a reconstruction workshop, I ran up against an intense emotional block in the star (the person who was seeking emotional healing). She was unable to do the actual emotional release work because she was medicated— and not in ways people might imagine. It was my first intense experience that taught me that nicotine was a drug that impaired the user from emotional healing. It was time to face this reality.

Our programs in the Black Hills consisted of groups of four to forty clients, counselors, and trainees who came to our facility for various programs each week. Our treatment programs were no-nonsense, intense, experiential psychotherapy (using Gestalt and psychodrama), education, and the building of self-worth. The group lived together in the Black Hills just beneath Mount Rushmore. It was a very spiritual and healing place to work.

In 1984, when this incident happened, I notified the sixty-five full-time and part-time employees that those on the Onsite staff who used nicotine in any form would be expected to be comfortably nicotine free in three months, by November of 1985. This would include administrative and clinical staff. Clients who were smokers were also told that the programs and facilities had become smoke free and that an ancillary support program and professional help for nicotine addiction were available to them. We sent out notices to all perspective clients saying that they had to either stop smoking before they came or they would be expected to stop upon arrival. Some did wait until they were comfortably free from nicotine before they signed up for a program, but most stopped the day they arrived. We then detoxed them and they began their emotional therapy with us. There was no other site; they were mixed in with the non-smokers and this in itself was help to all.

At that time Onsite and other treatment programs had not seriously addressed the problem of nicotine addiction directly. Other drug problems, including alcoholism, as well as eating disorders, and other mental health problems were more important and seemed to take precedence. Both the public perception and professional thinking was that the problem was "just smoking," not necessarily addiction. Many centers felt that alcoholism and other drug addictions were much more important to treat, "... don't take away their cigarettes and their drug/alcohol addiction at the same time ..."

Most staff and clients largely accepted my announcement with little disagreement. They knew it was a logical policy, but the smokers (staff and clients alike) were hesitant. They were not happy being caught in the change, but when they concentrated on nicotine dependence as a widespread and powerful addiction with many negative consequences, their resistance began to fade. The intensity of the emotional healing over eight days and the rapid detox with short-term or no nicotine replacement therapy allowed for most of the participants to return home, essentially out of withdrawal, comfortably free of nicotine. Their emotional pain had been released and the need for nicotine was much less of an issue. The results were quite encouraging. In addition to everyone pulling together for the "new non-smokers," the emotional involvement and the sharing between smokers and non-smokers added other dimensions to our programs.

Therapists were startled to find that those in nicotine withdrawal are more receptive to treatment than when they are "medicated" with nicotine. We saw amazing emotional wounds heal, and people able to deal with and release their cravings and make new decisions.

Our attempts to spread the word about our findings were met with resistance from treatment facilities. They were afraid of the effects on their business if smoking was not allowed. Rather than treating this addiction, they began to accommodate it by providing special areas and times when the nicotine addicts could take a break and go out to indulge in a cigarette.

They could then come back to therapy, medicated, just as my reconstruction star was.

I will be forever indebted to Dr. Joe Cruse for forging ahead in treating nicotine as a serious primary addiction and helping me prove that people can change and do successful emotional healing much quicker and much deeper as non-smokers. His book and companion work journal, *I Don't Smoke,* tells the whole story.

While the Onsite programs have been running successfully nicotine free since 1985, South Pacific Private Hospital in Sydney, Australia (working with Dr. Joe Cruse as consultant), is—thus far—the only treatment facility I know of to implement a complete nicotine abstinence policy. It took two years to accomplish and to get everyone on the same bandwagon.

LESSON LEARNED

Vision and perseverance are needed for social change to occur. As Thomas Carlyle said, "Permanence, perseverance and persistence, in spite of all obstacles, discouragements and impossibilities: It is this, that in all things distinguishes the strong soul from the weak."

Coupleship Programs

*"Coupleship means a passionate, spiritual, emotional, and sexual
commitment between two people that nourishes both."*
—Sharon Wegscheider-Cruse

The success of the reconstruction process in providing a life-changing process for the single person known as the "star" led to the following idea popping into my head. What if I facilitated two of these processes at the same time for a couple, and they could be involved in each other's therapeutic process? Invitations went out to twenty couples who might consider this process. All twenty signed up, and we suddenly had forty people in what we called the "couples program."

The problem started when, after doing exhausting and intensive interviewing, one of the people prepared became seriously ill and needed to be hospitalized. Each of these couples was attending from a different state, and they were now registered and housed in our treatment setting. We had hoped to do two reconstructions working with one couple. They had prepared for about two months for that experience. The other nineteen couples were going to watch and role play in that couple's work; they were not prepared to do emotional work except by observance of watching the star couple.

What to do? We sat down at our dining room table and talked it over with two couples that were going to work with us. On the spot, we wrote a whole new and different program. We changed it from a dual reconstruction to a couples program and proceeded the next morning with all new plans. We had all the couples do their own emotional work in one big group plus smaller therapy groups. Today, that model we wrote in one night still happens at Onsite in Tennessee. It has stood the test of more than twenty-five years and still helps couples enrich their relationships.

Some couples come because they are facing a major hurdle in their relationship, some come because they are planning a divorce and want to avoid conflicts for their children, some come because they are thinking about getting married, and some come because their parents have already done the program and they give it to the new bride and groom to give them a head start. No matter what the reason, they get their needs met.

LESSONS LEARNED

Even when we think we are doing the work the universe asks of us, our plans are always up in the air and made for us by divine intervention. The coupleship program was literally handed to us as we sat around the dining room table with staff and friends. We had a whole different plan going which was not to be. God provides. For thirty years this program has brought hope and help to countless couples.

Living Centered Program

*"We can choose to function at a lower level of
awareness and simply exist taking care of our possessions,
eating, drinking, sleeping, and managing our affairs.
Or we can soar to higher levels of awareness allowing ourselves
to transcend our environment and literally create a world
of our own—a world of real magic."*

—Wayne W. Dyer

What became clear in the reconstructions was that many people needed more time, therapy, and more than the reconstruction could provide in that time frame. In addition, many of the attendees found they also wanted more work. Back then there were no stand-alone codependency-intensive programs. Something was very much needed.

With Joe's knowledge of treatment, that became his role at Onsite. What he developed was an outpatient, live-together model that fit our setting. People would fly in from all over the country and live together in the motel we leased. I hired a nighttime supervisor who would live in the motel with them.

We chose five group leaders to come in and live at our home; they provided therapy during the day. Since they were with us for only eight days, we also held programs in the evenings. Each day was close to a fourteen-hour workday. The amount of actual therapy for an attendee was almost the same number of hours that addicts and alcoholics were getting in twenty-eight to thirty-day programs.

The Living Centered Program (LCP) he developed was magical and very successful, thanks to Joe's dedication and creativity. The same program continues, thirty years later, in Tennessee. It was a win for us and for attendees.

Month after month, since November 1985, forty new people have continued to attend this program, finding inner peace, strength, self-worth, and hope. In a ripple effect, each of those forty lives changed positively impacts four more lives. Nice legacy! Thank you, Joe.

LESSONS LEARNED

Joe taught me many lessons. He insisted on combining the specificity of medical programs with the healing mysticism of spiritual programs. He found the magic design, and thirty years later, this program is the core of Onsite. His top concern was always protecting the client and ensuring safety. I wanted to be the mystic and he insisted on being the scientist. The combination was magical.

Twelve Steps of Recovery

"A 'miracle' is an event that appears unexplainable by laws
of nature and so is held to be an act of God."

—Sharon Wegscheider-Cruse

Originally, Onsite programs were a combination of classic therapy modalities, spirituality, healing, and the twelve steps of recovery. The twelve steps, published in 1939, were written to help alcoholics stay sober. The method has become the foundation for many other twelve-step programs. There are now more than 200 self-help organizations that use these steps, including: drug groups, overeating groups, sex-addiction groups, gambling groups, etc. No self-help program has equaled the recovery success in the same way the twelve-step way of life has.

The Twelve Steps

1) We admitted that we were powerless over alcohol—that our lives had become unmanageable.
2) Came to believe that a Power greater than ourselves could restore us to sanity.
3) Made a decision to turn our will and our lives over to the care of God *as we understood Him.*
4) Made a searching and fearless moral inventory of ourselves.
5) Admitted to God, to ourselves, and to another human being the exact nature of our wrongs.
6) Were entirely ready to have God remove all these defects of character.
7) Humbly asked Him to remove our shortcomings.
8) Made a list of all persons we had harmed, and became willing to make amends to them all.

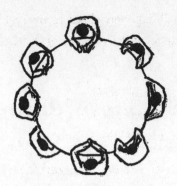

9) Made direct amends to such people wherever possible, except when to do so would injure them or others.

10) Continued to take personal inventory and when we were wrong, promptly admitted it.

11) Sought through prayer and meditation to improve our conscious contact with God, *as we understood Him*, praying only for knowledge of His will for us and the power to carry that out.

12) Having had a spiritual awakening as the result of these Steps, we tried to carry this message to alcoholics, and to practice these principles in all our affairs.[1]

These steps became the foundation of my recovery. They have brought me peace, comfort, and hope. Living by them has been the best recovery I could possibly have. However, I needed to change the word God to Higher Power and not use the word Him. I also was not an alcoholic, my parents were, so I changed the word alcoholic to people pleaser and it worked for me. It's a great way to live in general.

Then one night on the way to be a co-keynote speaker with Father Joseph C. Martin, a speaker, priest, and star of the classic film *Chalk Talk*, we were in

---

1 The Twelve Steps are reprinted with permission of Alcoholics Anonymous World Services, Inc. ("AAWS"). Permission to reprint the Twelve Steps does not mean that AAWS has reviewed or approved the contents of this publication, or that AAWS necessarily agrees with the views expressed herein. A.A. is a program of recovery from alcoholism *only*—use of the Twelve Steps in connection with programs and activities which are patterned after A.A., but which address other problems, or in any other non-A.A. context, does not imply otherwise.

the back of a limo and talking away about recovery. He said to me, "Sharon, you don't have to be so specific. I use the shortcut and it works for me." The shortcut is:

The first four steps are: Trust God.
The next four steps are: Clean House.
The last four steps are: Help Others.

Bingo! How clear is that? The first four and the last four had been a part of my life since treatment. However, I had some housecleaning to do and it was hard. Over the next six months, I cleaned my house and nothing has been the same since. Now I review the shortcuts about once a month and do what I have to do.

LESSONS LEARNED

One cannot improve on the wisdom of the Twelve Steps of recovery. They say it all.

The National Association for Children of Alcoholics

"You are never given a dream without also
being given the power to make it true.
You will work for it, however."

—Richard Bach

In the early seventies, four of us were trying hard to bring the needs of children of alcoholics to the forefront of recovery: Claudia Black, Cathleen Brooks, Stephanie Brown, and myself. We were in different parts of the country and had never met. I was also trying to get Joe Cruse to see how important family issues were to the field of addiction. He decided to hold a conference for medical professionals at the Annenberg Center in Palm Desert, and invited all four of us to meet and speak.

It was quite a historic moment when we all met as Joe was showing us how to work the media station. Then we took off and each presented our best. Family advocates were not all that welcome in those days and having each other's support was such a good feeling.

Little did we know that philanthropist Joan Kroc, who inherited the fortune of Ray Kroc, CEO of McDonald's, had flown in to hear us. When we finished she came up to meet us, insisting that we had important information that the world needed to know. She offered to bring us to her ranch in Santa Barbara, all expenses paid, to brainstorm for a weekend and come up with an idea of how to get this vital information out. We met at the Kroc Ranch shortly afterwards and spent a whole weekend getting to know each other. Sadly, we did not come up with a plan; we were more interested in meeting each other and listening to each other's stories.

Instead of being disappointed, she completely understood and gave us a task. She said she would support and finance a second weekend, and this time she expected results. She said we could each bring two more people we trusted to be part of this task force. I went back to Minnesota and chose Bob Subby, a therapist, healer, and author of *Lost in the Shuffle*, and Rokelle Lerner, a therapist, healer, and author of *Affirmations*. We convened again on February 14, 1982 and spent the whole week working on the plan. When we finished, we had organized the National Association for Children of Alcoholics (NACoA) with the mission of bringing information, connection, and hope to all children of alcoholics. It was my honor to be the first chairman of the board, and we became the founding board of directors.

NACoA's mission is to eliminate the adverse impact of alcohol and drug use on children and families.

LESSONS LEARNED

There were so many lessons from NACoA. One of my biggest personal lessons was realizing that even as a professional and an adult, the impact of alcoholism was very much still with me. I had more healing to do.

Another lesson was how much I grew to love this dedicated group of men and women who, even though they too had been affected, were willing to focus their careers on bringing this organization to the forefront and doing whatever they could to help children from alcoholic families.

This lesson, that a few caring people could make such a significant difference, will stay with me forever.

Lady in the Red Dress

*"Nearly all the best things that came to me in my life
have been unexpected, unplanned by me."*
—Carl Sandburg

While filming *The Family Trap*, I wore a solid red shirtdress. The movie was about the roles I developed as part of the treatment and training programs: the Family Hero, the Scapegoat, the Lost Child, and the Mascot. It was shown in treatment and mental-health centers, and in counselors' offices.

A family that had been in a treatment program was flying home from the session and had a layover in a hotel where I happened to be staying. By coincidence, if you believe it, I was wearing the red dress from the film. As I went for a Starbucks coffee, I heard a little boy's voice saying, "Hey lady, hey lady!" I turned around and there was a boy about eight years old. I said, "Yes, what can I do for you?" He answered, "I think you are the *Family Trap* lady I saw in the film at the treatment center." He was so excited, it warmed my heart. Telling him he was right made both of us happy.

"I am always the lost child at home and in school," he explained. "After you said that, it made me lonely. I knew it was true, so I decided to speak up and come talk to you. I'm going to do it at home as well as at school. I don't have to be lost if I don't want to be. Thanks."

He stepped out of the shadow of the lost child that day, and it's my hope that he never went into the shadow again.

LESSONS LEARNED

This little boy taught me that we often do not know the impact we have on each other. His courage to come and talk to a stranger, even though he knew me from the film, made the whole trip worthwhile for me.

Authors and filmmakers often do not know their impact on readers and watchers. My lesson is to keep producing. whether you know the results or not.

Mystical Happenings: Danny

*"Trust is the glue of life. It's the most essential ingredient
in effective communication. It's the foundational
principle that holds all relationships."*

—Stephen Covey

To protect family privacy, the name of the person at the heart of this story has been changed to Danny. He came to one of our programs to process his feelings about the fact that he was getting married again after a divorce, but his family was not welcoming his new bride. Danny made friends with his group and felt an acceptance he appreciated. After being in the program for close to six days, the group took a hike in the woods behind our center. Danny had a massive heart attack and died right on the spot.

This was our only tragedy in our thirty-plus years. He had listed his parents as next of kin as he had not yet remarried. They came to our center and thanked us because Danny had told them during his time in the program that he had never been so happy. They took his body home, we had a ceremony with his group at the site where he died, and the experience ended at that time.

About nine years later, we were on a cruise somewhere near the Philippines. It was a very long cruise and I decided to take a two-week yoga class on the ship. My teacher was a beautiful and delightful lady. One day I thanked her for such a good class and she asked where I was from. I said Rapid City, South Dakota, and she said, "Oh my God, my fiancé died in Rapid City." We talked further and discovered that her fiancé was Danny. We emailed his group leader from back then, who told her about Danny's last few days. The leader was able to bring closure to nine years of "unfinished business" for her. It was a blessing.

LESSONS LEARNED

The major lesson I learned is that the universe/power of God is so much bigger than me. How could a happening in South Dakota affecting a man from the eastern United States connect up with me on a cruise in the Philippines? No one could make up this story. Trust. Believe.

Favorite Group-Leader Stories

"A strong social network is foundational."
—Jim Harter, coauthor of
Wellbeing: The Five Essential Elements

One of our group leaders was constantly dealing with shyness. He used to say he sometimes felt like wallpaper, just there. He was a good therapist but had difficulty asking to have his own needs met. Each time he was in a program, we all gave him tools, suggestions, and homework to make himself reach out and speak out.

Locked In

One morning we finished meditation, and two cars of group leaders headed to the program center. There was lots of chatter and laughter on the way, and then each leader went to his or her assigned group. It wasn't until the program actually started that someone from his group came to me to say he was missing. This was before cell phones, and our house had dead bolt locks inside and out. He was locked in our house, we didn't have a house phone, and nobody had noticed he wasn't with us.

It was only after a half hour ride back to Crestwood to get him that we learned that he had gone to the bathroom and each car thought he was in the other car. The day came when he could talk and laugh about it.

Christmas, Hanukkah, Easter, and Birthdays

Many of our group leaders have grown up in painful homes. Many children of trauma, addiction, and workaholism have entered the helping professions to try to help or understand their own families. The intimacy of the hot tub brought out many stories of difficult holidays in their childhood homes. So we tried to celebrate every holiday when the group leaders were there to build a new memory bank. How I remember the songs played on our piano, singing, wrapping presents, playing in the snow, playing horseshoes and volleyball in the summer. Many new family connections of choice were made at Crestwood.

Arrival Dinner

The night before the programs started, we'd have a couple of airport runs to pick up the group leaders. Janice, our cook, would prepare a Thanksgiving dinner with all the trimmings. Each incoming visitor would have her or his name on the bedroom door, a bathrobe waiting, and a welcoming Thanksgiving dinner. There were always fresh flowers by the bedside. Each visit was a special time for them and we tried to be the welcoming parents, no matter the age of the group leader. It was a psychological "welcome home."

Sturgis, South Dakota Motorcycle Rally

In August of each year, it was important to invite group leaders with a sense of adventure. In the Black Hills, hundreds of thousands of Harley-Davidson riders descend on the little town of Sturgis nearby for the annual motorcycle rally. Usually, the last night we would take the staff to the heart of the rally. First, we'd put removable tattoos in all the right places, don our leather clothes and silver jewelry, and drive to about one-half mile from Sturgis, park our cars and head into town. No one really knew there wasn't a single Harley rider in our crowd. We would visit tattoo parlors, music jams, and food vendors, becoming part of the crowd. We had some mighty interesting adventures.

Add to these adventures countless bedtime stories, visiting the site of the movie *Dances with Wolves* to see the herds of buffalo, hiking the hills, popcorn and movies at night, and all the experiences we shared enabled many (including me) to build a lifetime of "family" stories in those years. It was a magical time and many miracles happened.

LESSONS LEARNED

It is through love, trust, and respect that healing happens. My life was enriched through these group leaders, and I hold their names, their lives, and their contributions in my heart and soul. We never know where our family will come from; we were a strong, loving group of peers who became family.

Marty Mann Award

"Awards can give you a tremendous amount of encouragement to keep getting better, no matter how young or old you are."

—Alan Alda

Marty Mann was an early member of Alcoholics Anonymous and is often remembered as the person who helped move the perception of alcoholism away from the stigma of a moral failing and into a health issue.. She fought against common ignorance about alcoholism and worked to encourage acceptance of the "disease model." In 1944 she founded the National Council on Alcoholism and Drug Dependence (NCADD).

Three ideas were at the core of her message:

1) Alcoholism is a disease and the alcoholic is a sick person.
2) The alcoholic can be helped and is worth helping.
3) Alcoholism is a public health problem and therefore a public responsibility.

Some have said she was the greatest contributor to reducing the stigma of alcoholism. Her national fame was cemented when NCADD hosted Operation Understanding, NCADD's Challenge to Stigma.

In 1981 Father Joseph C. Martin was given the first Marty Mann Award for his contribution to the field of alcoholism through his film, *Chalk Talk*.

In 1982 I was the first woman to receive the Marty Mann Award as top communicator in the field for that year, and for my book, *Another Chance*. It was a great honor.

Here is the rest of the story. Much earlier I was the first non-alcoholic to speak about the needs of the family in a national conference sponsored by the National Council on Alcoholism, then known as NCA. Many people there did not welcome me as they thought if we worried too much or knew too much about the family issues, it would make it harder and more difficult for the alcoholic. Males dominated the field at that time, and they were none too welcoming of female "rabble-rousers," as family therapists were known.

For me to chair a major section at the conference was quite controversial. However, a wonderful pioneer in the field, Geraldine O. Delaney of Little Hill-Alina Lodge in Blairstown, New Jersey, was a board member. She raised a huge fuss and I was invited. (If you happened to note her initials, they were on a wooden sign that marked her reserved spot in the parking lot: GOD.)

When I arrived at my hotel in Washington, DC, I was a bit nervous. I was led to my session room in the basement of the hotel where the conference was held. The room held about fifty people and was behind the furnace room and uncomfortably hot.

Upstairs there were about ten spacious rooms, each of which could hold about 200 people. Each of the upstairs rooms also had coffee and water in the back of the room and cushioned folding chairs. My room had no refreshments and card table chairs. All sessions were piped through the speaker system throughout the hotel.

The day began. Even before my presentation started, the room was packed, with people standing around the edges. As I began my talk, people started sitting on the steps leading to the lower level. We could hardly breathe because of the crowd and the heat. Suddenly, a man jumped up and said, "This is ridiculous. We need space and air. Hold that talk."

I continued, but he went to the hotel management who were shocked to see all the people sitting on the steps and the floor. The man's name was Bob Haven and he was director of Twin Town Treatment Center in St. Paul, Minnesota.

He arranged with the management to take over connecting upper suites on the top floor of the hotel, and people took out pencils and paper and wrote protest signs. Here are a few examples: Families Need Help, Families Count, and Children of Alcoholics Hurt. All of the audience then marched through the hotel, past all the other conference rooms, and took over the top of the hotel. Water and coffee was provided. I never did know if the hotel provided it or if he had paid for it. But it was spectacular.

During the reprise of my talk in the upper rooms, there was a knock on the door. A lady was wheeled in and pushed right up to my podium. I thought I was in big trouble. She asked for the microphone, and when I gave it to her she said, "Hello Sharon, I am Marty Mann and I want to thank you for your contribution to the field of addiction. Your work is an example of why I started the National Council on Alcoholism. These are the words alcoholics need to hear." I was stunned, honored, and left a bit speechless.

Years later I was honored to be the first woman to receive the Marty Mann Award.

LESSON LEARNED

Once again, the universe is at work. This lesson is about serendipity and coincidence, for those who believe in coincidence. My work in the field was so much more recent than Marty Mann's, and yet she showed up at my workshop to give me her total support. God works in wondrous ways.

Jerry Florence, My First Musical Sage

"When we use one sense, it is noted and used.
When we use additional senses, there is more imprinting
with sight, sound, hearing, touch, and taste. The more pathways that
are firing at the same time, the greater the impact. Music often
is our biggest impact, maybe most when we are young and old.
In the middle we stay too busy."

—Virginia Satir

There were many angels at work in my work and I hope I have mentioned most of them. Jerry Florence was a major angel.

My love of public speaking made me very excited to be making a special presentation in Seattle, Washington. The subject was spirituality and recovery, two of my favorite topics. There were about 1,100 people in the crowd, which made it even more thrilling. I spent many nights preparing, developing a script and slides, and arranging for a special musical ending.

There was a sparkle in the air looking out on the city and the Space Needle as all the bright lights started to twinkle. Right across the street, the message on a convention center marquee jumped out at me: "Incredible Hulk has a sell-out crowd of 26,000." My 1,100 suddenly seemed small. For a minute, my whole presentation felt small. However, I said my favorite prayer and told my God that I'd do my best and would love to have a sign that it was going well. Following me was going to be live music with a group called Go With the Flow.

It all went great, the audience was warm and welcoming, and it felt like the presentation was well received. Toward the end, the lighting technician was preparing to dim the lights as I announced that we were going to listen to "Amazing Grace" on tape, and then sing it together.

The room was completely dark when I pressed the recorder for the song to start. There was nothing. Incredulous, I pressed again—nothing. Panicking, I pressed again. Just before asking the technician to bring up the lights, there was a noise as someone came on stage. I was frozen. I felt a hand on my hand and heard someone say, "It's all right."

Less than a minute later, I heard an amazing voice begin to play the keyboard in the dark and start to sing "Amazing Grace." It was the dearest, pure voice I had ever heard. When he finished, the audience began to sing with him one more time. Slowly the lights began to come up and there was Jerry Florence, playing his keyboard. Eleven-hundred voices were singing along. My sign had been sent.

That was when I first met Jerry, and that changed my life. He traveled with my company and me for several years, singing in my workshops and presentations. He was an angel.

LESSONS LEARNED

I was fortunate enough to meet an angel. Jerry was an angel to many, but he taught me to be available and say yes. He said yes to me in so many ways, not knowing what the outcome would be. He taught me gentleness, the importance of diversity, what it is to struggle against prejudice and hypocrisy, to stand up for my own beliefs, and total love.

Lace Afghan from the Homeless

"Be kind whenever possible. It is always possible."

—Dalai Lama

Years ago I traveled to Los Angeles on a regular basis and presented workshops for two or three recovery programs. The director of the Salvation Army attended one program. He came up to me afterward and told me his plight. He said that there were many homeless people who could very much benefit from my information about the family illness of addiction, but they could never afford to bring me to speak to them. I offered to volunteer.

That started my tradition of adding a day onto each of my paid trips to take the time to go down to the part of L.A. where homeless people gathered. He would gather the people, and I would share with them. This was part of my regular schedule for more than a year. When my contracts with the recovery centers ended, it brought an end to my work with the homeless.

On my last visit, three of the ladies who were "homeless regulars" in my program presented me with a beautiful lace afghan they had knitted for me. They had collected money from the others in the group who were also homeless regulars and bought the yarn. The three of them worked on it. It is a beautiful piece of work.

It washes like a towel and holds its shape. I believe that it also holds spiritual energy. When I feel overtired or even ill, it wraps me in the love of that group of people. Their love for me will remain with me forever.

LESSONS LEARNED

Too often, those who have much to give, give little, and those who have little, give so much. This afghan will be with me forever and continue to share its spiritual energy. Whenever tired or ill, my lesson has been that there is great energy in it.

Retirement or Redirection

"I can change the story. I am the story."
—Jeanette Winterson

The day I heard my first grandson cry I decided it was time for me to retire or redirect. Working had been my lifestyle and brought order, meaning, and financial safety. My children had sacrificed along with me to make the dream of recovery for alcoholic families possible. It had all happened, and it was time for me to find meaning and satisfaction in other ways.

My children were still my greatest joy, and now my first grandchild offered me hope that there would be more connections and love. I had missed out on too many things with my own children. Yet working was necessary financially, and fulfilling a mission for alcoholic families was a strong drive. This was a second chance for me and taking it was very important.

Part of me knew there probably never would be a full retirement. But some of the people involved with my public speaking were convinced I would always be there. And for many years, I continued to speak. It was the last to go. However, the commitment to my grandchildren was cemented inside.

Selling Onsite meant the end of an era for me and was very hard to do. There were a couple of false starts, but the custodians of this special program appeared and the transition went totally smoothly. They took over; basically, I simply disappeared. There was never a blip in the service and programs offered. For me, it was like seeing one of my children marry or move away. It was a huge loss, but one I was ready for. The year was 1995, and we moved to Las Vegas.

LESSON LEARNED

The lesson was it was time and it was enough. One thing that was clear to me was that I did not know how to enjoy leisure and just "be." Selling Onsite might be the beginning of knowing what it meant to stop "doing" and "just be."

Jobs Versus Careers

"The place God calls you to is the place where your deep
gladness and the world's deep hunger meet."
—Frederick Buechner

I felt finished.

I have never applied for a job since my early twenties. I only have had careers. What's the difference? To me, a job is something we do for a certain number of hours for someone else and we can count on a paycheck for the job done or the hours spent on that job.

A career, on the other hand, is more like a calling or a mission. We do what we do because we want to do it. It's a bonus when we can get a paycheck for it at the same time.

For me, finding a way to help alcoholics and their families was truly my mission. It was something that drove me until it became my career. In the early days, it took money just to be able to do what I needed to do. It was costly to barely make it financially while my dream was to do what became my job later on.

It was a risky choice. It would have been much easier (but much less satisfying) to take a job and know a paycheck was coming every week. But my heart wasn't in it. I needed to do what I had to do, and it made all the difference. My personal road less traveled took me to places I didn't even know existed.

It wasn't always done right; there were failures and uncertainty. If we want to accomplish something that has never been done before, we have to experiment and that means taking a risk. It might not be done perfectly. An old Japanese proverb teaches us, "Fall down seven, stand up eight." Many times I felt that way.

Once when my group therapy for five-year-olds wasn't working, a fire truck went by, and they all jumped up and ran to the window to see what was happening. I was going to scold them, bring them back, and start my lesson again. However, they charmed me and I decided to wait until the experience passed. When they sauntered back and got into the group circle, I gave each of them a treat for having the courage to follow their curiosity, and we turned that into a lesson.

It's always been important for me to remember the questions posed by the Jewish sage, Hillel the Elder. "If not us, who? If not now, when?"

Who knows? I may add to my career, but I will never have a job.

LESSON LEARNED

As I sold Onsite, I realized that my time there had never felt like a job for me. My work in the field of addictions, family therapy, and building community had always felt like a mission. A job is something that you start, you contribute, and when you are finished, you leave. A passion or a mission stays with you forever. That kind of career is harder to leave.

All Teachings Are the Same

"This is my simple religion.
There is no need for temples, no need for
complicated philosophy. Our own brain, our own heart
is our temple. The philosophy is kindness."

—Dalai Lama

Even though life was very busy, I continued to learn when and where I could. Attending workshops and intensives were my major source of learning. The more things I studied, the more I found out that all teachings are very similar. I saw this Zen saying on a wall and it spoke to me: "When your vision is clear, all great teachings are the same." From the perch of this time of my life, I find great truth in this saying.

I first thought about it on my trip around the world. There were truths that I experienced in each country. Regardless of the culture, many things were the same. Young children in different schools were somewhat the same. They laughed, they ran, they played, they giggled, and they had fun. Each culture had mothers who showed their love for their children.

In my many years as a mother, grandmother, friend, therapist, entrepreneur, author, and public speaker, there were consistent reminders that what most people continued to want and pursue was connection in relationships, something meaningful to do, self-respect and self-worth, and someone to hold their hand when afraid. Most of all, they wanted someone to listen. There is no big mystery about being a helpful and good therapist. People's needs are often quite simple.

In the programs at Onsite, some therapists were addiction counselors; some were psychiatrists, psychologists, social workers, and pastors. They each had to have some path they had chosen and become skilled and proficient in.

However, just as important to us, they needed to demonstrate that they lived a balanced and healthy lifestyle. We were the first program in the seventies that did not hire therapists who smoked. If they had addiction issues, they needed to be in a recovery program for at least two years prior to training with us. If an eating disorder was present, they needed to be in recovery for that as well.

Virginia Satir had taught me to never be a technician or a copycat person. She didn't have much interest in guru followers and laid a foundation for me in my own career. She always told me to be an original thinker and doer and to use my creativity, and not to be a follower that sought out more and more of the "latest" modalities. She said, "You can always be a first-class innovator, but only a second-class follower."

One of my friends who wrote a book about money interviewed me and asked, "How do you know when you have enough money to retire?" It made me think, how do any of us know when we have learned enough about anything in this life? It's a great relief for me to know when something is *enough*. For me, it is now and my soul is quiet. I know I will always be a lifetime learner. I am curious, interested, and open to new ideas. But I have stopped being a seeker. I love this saying from *Jonathan Livingston Seagull* by Richard Bach: "It's good to be a seeker. But sooner or later, you have to be a finder.

And then it is well to give what you have found, a gift into the world for whoever will accept it."

My heart has found contentment, my mind feels creative, and I am beginning to harvest my life's work, personally and professionally.

What I craved most during my working days was time. Sometimes, my schedule was booked two years in advance. It had to be that way for some organizations and groups. If they really wanted me as a keynote speaker and I wanted to do it, it was usually at least a year to ensure a date. When that happened frequently, my schedule would fill two years in advance. It became my lifestyle, but it didn't allow for much spontaneity. I craved mornings when I could wake up and not have to go to the airport or start a local program. Time has become a treasure.

LESSONS LEARNED

Even if I was not ready, I learned it was time to stop. In my career, the lesson was that when all is said and done, there is just so much truth in the world and coming to that point is different for each person and each culture. However, it all is the same at some level, and once it's known, that's all there is. Life is really quite simple, once you know. At that time, I knew that my similarities in life were bigger than my differences. I could rest. My karmic duty was done. Now I could "be— not just "do."

Chapter Seven

LAS VEGAS

Culture Change:
Learning How Not to Work

"Good judgment comes from experience.
Experience comes from bad judgment."
—Rita Mae Brown

When we left the serenity of the Black Hills to move to Las Vegas, Nevada in 1995, it surprised many of our friends and peers. Yet it was the right thing to do. We had a small condo there and enjoyed a month or two in the winter during our really busy years. Joe had retired, but I was still working.

It was such a contrast to all that I had lived and done in recent years. It felt like I had been working all my life. Actually, I had been working since I was seventeen. I loved my work and it had brought me an interesting and meaningful lifestyle. Because I so loved my work, much of my work had also been my play. My staff were my friends. Each day flew by and most of the time I was filled with satisfaction and joy, even when I was exhausted.

Las Vegas was what I needed after a life of output. It felt like continuous vacation, and it took energy just to get used to it. It was brand new to me and different to have choices about what to do with my time—especially to choose something that was not productive. The feeling was strange, visceral, and foreign.

I wasn't sure I knew how to "not work." In the early years in Vegas, I was still making airline runs and still traveling to conferences and workshops. I became a consultant to a treatment center for a year. And I kept writing, which I have always loved. Not working seemed impossible.

Las Vegas was the perfect city in which to begin questioning my lifestyle. In many ways, Las Vegas served as an intervention on workaholism after nearly four decades of constant output.

It became clear that I needed to teach myself how to enjoy leisure time, and where better than Las Vegas, where there is so much to experience? I entertained, hosted, read, was entertained, connected, lunched, explored, shopped, played games, exercised, and found a part of myself that had been undiscovered in many years of working. Travel became a value; before, it had been part of work. Now it became an end in itself.

One of my fantasies was to become a tap dancer. Loving music and ballroom dancing my way through high school brought me soul-filling memories; music has always been a passion. I spent fifteen years taking tap dancing and enjoying the learning and the fun of it. In Las Vegas I performed in shows, but that felt too much like my working days. However, those years of tapping were a great joy. Cynthia Hemel says, "When in doubt, make a fool

of yourself. There is only a microscopically thin line between being brilliantly creative and acting like an idiot. So, what the hell? *Leap!*"

Gardening is another true love. My thirty rose bushes brought me great joy. So did other plants, indoor and outdoor. My creativity got a great boost with entertaining. Sometimes, my guests didn't know if they were in a workshop or at a party, but we all had so much fun.

Las Vegas entertainment is the best and I learned to take advantage of it all. Families and friends came to visit and our home was always open. Coming from Minnesota, I didn't know if I could learn to love the beauty of the desert, but I did.

I have never lived anywhere as long as I lived in Las Vegas, so the friendships and long-term involvement in a community brought me great satisfaction. I took all the time I needed to nurture those friendships; they will last my entire life.

LESSONS LEARNED

I relearned the lesson about the trials and victories of making a big move. We had tested Las Vegas and knew we were going to like it there. My lessons had taught me that I needed to learn how to relax and enjoy leisure, and there is no place better for that than Las Vegas.

I learned how to make friends without work being involved. I learned that every day could feel like Sunday. I learned how to tap dance and perform in front of audiences. This was very different from speaking to audiences. I loved them both.

My roses were also another wonderful experience for me. I learned to plant, weed, prune, and fertilize. It's a great metaphor for life.

Timeless Time

"The person who says it cannot be done must
not interrupt the person doing it."
—Chinese Proverb

For much of my life, time was a precious gift and I had way too little of it for myself. Going to school, working, maintaining a home, running a business —and the list goes on and on. It seemed that I was often left wanting time to do things that were important to me, but usually time ran out.

Somewhere along the way, while scheduling the days, weeks, and sometimes years, it became clear to me that *my* life needed scheduling as well. Taking a red pen, I put in the time I needed. I scheduled exercise, shopping and errands, and anything else important to me. Then and only then did I schedule other commitments. I called those blocks of totally unscheduled time for me my "timeless time."

When someone asked for my available time, all my "timeless time" was already on my calendar in red and I simply answered, "I'm already booked." It was true since I had now counted myself in.

This style became very important as I redirected. The assumption was made that I had all free time. That was so not true. It still is one of my best self-care choices.

LESSON LEARNED

What I've learned about "timeless time" is that it works. My red-marking "time for myself" has guaranteed that frenzy rarely happens to me. There is time for the people in my life that I care about and there is time for me.

Time is as valuable as money. We get twenty-four hours a day and that's it. Take away the time we sleep, eat, dress and manage clothes, drive, shop, run errands, manage finances, and keep medical and legal appointments. The rest is time for us to use as we decide. If we don't schedule timeless time, many of our needs don't get met. This method really works for me.

The Minnesota Vikings

"The moments of happiness we enjoy take us by surprise.
It is not that we seize them, but they seize us."
—Ashley Montagu

This is the story of my grandson, who is a totally committed Minnesota Vikings fan. He lives in Alaska and follows their games on TV. Loving the game of football and the sibling rivalry with his brothers, one a Green Bay Packers fan and the other a Philadelphia Eagles fan, he is devoted to his team.

He is such a fan that he started an Internet site to follow player drafts, scores, and stories about the Vikings. This has gone on for years. His website and followers caught the eye of a sports reporter who wanted to interview this obscure fan in Alaska.

The article appeared in the *Minneapolis Star Tribune,* where the former chairman of the board of my company, Onsite, saw it. He thought he recognized the name and called to ask if that was my grandson. Upon hearing that it was, he asked if he had ever seen a Vikings game live. No, he had not.

My chairman was a former owner of the Vikings. He proceeded to tell me that if I could get him and his Packers rival to Minnesota, he would produce tickets. For two high school kids from Alaska, a trip to Minnesota to see the Vikings sounded wonderful. We were also invited and so were my Minnesota grandchildren. Within the week, we came from Las Vegas, the boys came from Alaska, and everyone was excited about the game. Joe and I met with my friend to pick up the tickets. Over lunch, he simply said, "Come in door number seven and give them my name. Come early." We did so and were ushered into the stadium and down a long hall.

The usher opened the door and we were brought into the owner's box! What a treat. There were comfortable seats, a waitress to meet all our needs, very good food, and a large sliding window between the field and us. In all, there was just my family, my chairman of the board, and Sally and George Pillsbury. The boys were amazed and overwhelmed. We had a few snacks and then received our VIP badges and were taken down to the field where they got to meet some of their Viking heroes. It was surreal—very much like a dream come true for the boys.

They met the owners and sportscasters as well as many of the players. They will never forget that day and neither will I.

On the way out of the stadium, the sports writer who did the original story called my grandson on his cell phone and interviewed him again about the experience and wrote another article. Later that week, back in Las Vegas and relishing this rich time, I received a call from the Vikings office wanting my grandson's home address. A couple of weeks later, he received a final gift: a football helmet signed by the Vikings.

LESSON LEARNED

Things happen out of nowhere. I learned to "seize the moment." We had an opportunity and a chance to do something that might never come together again. Therefore, we put a bookmark in our daily lives and experienced the whole event. None of us will ever forget the fun and the excitement of this time together.

President Gerald Ford's Funeral

"I love life. I think it's fantastic.
Sometimes it deals hard things, and when it deals
great things, you have to seize them."

—Sam Taylor-Wood

We heard on the radio that President Gerald Ford had died. Knowing him as we did through our association with his wife, Betty, we felt badly and were trying to think of how to honor him. At breakfast, the phone rang. Imagine my surprise when I heard the following: "Good morning, this is the White House and I am looking to reach either Joe or Sharon Cruse."

The White House representative had called to invite us to Washington, DC for President Ford's funeral. We accepted on the spot. I listened to the instructions about times, hotel arrangements, security, and what they needed from us, hung up, and we prepared to leave in two days.

Having been to the capital several times, we found the funeral week a totally different experience. Right from the airport, it was as though a hush had fallen over the city. Cars were quieter, cabs were quieter, and people were quieter. Regardless of politics and preferences, there was a respect for the presidency that was part of the fabric of the city. We could hear it, see it, and feel it.

Each event we attended had the same subdued air. We took the walk through the rotunda to pay our respects, seeing people we usually see only on TV, and walking in and out of the hotel. We felt elevated to a different planet. One of the couples we ran into were George and Sally Pillsbury, whom we had just seen at the Minnesota Vikings game.

We saw some of President Ford's children on the sidewalk and had a chance to share stories. Betty Ford called our room and told us she was happy that we came. From the beginning, we knew we had done the right thing to drop everything and just come.

Nothing, however, prepared me for the funeral itself. We were seated at Washington National Cathedral two hours before the actual event. Security was very tight. Looking around was an extraordinary experience. The mixture of politicians, many seeming to walk out of my television set and into the room, and celebrities together with world leaders was disorienting. It was like a history book, television show, and a movie all happening at once. We sat across from Larry King, whom I watched most evenings at that time.

When the former presidents and First Ladies came in, the air crackled with awe and power. There was President Jimmy Carter and Rosalynn, President George H. W. Bush and Barbara, Laura Bush, Nancy Reagan, and President Bill Clinton and Hillary.

There was the United States Marine Orchestra, the Armed Forces Chorus, archbishops, rabbis, leaders from around the world, and five-star generals. Members from both houses of Congress were seated just behind us. Once everyone was seated, President George W. Bush brought Betty Ford down the aisle. From beginning to end, we were awestruck by the ceremony, the respect, and the wonder of it all. We had a chance to visit with Sam Donaldson, Madeleine Albright, and David Hartman of *Good Morning America*.

That whole weekend, there was a feeling of pride in the United States of America. It all felt real and like you could touch history. It wasn't all in history books and on television or in the newspapers. It was alive, touchable, and available. Never before or since have I felt so proud of being an American.

LESSONS LEARNED

I was honored to be part of another great "seize the moment" event. In retrospect, this was one of the greatest historical events I have ever experienced. We did not take the time to think about it. The call came and we said yes immediately. Missing it would have left a big vacuum in my appreciation of history. I learned that I was very patriotic and was honored to be part of this sacred time.

The Giraffes

"We evolve at the rate of the tribe
we are plugged in to."
—Caroline Myss

More than twenty-five years ago, seven women decided to share their lives with each other on a regular basis. They planned to have a weekend in Las Vegas each year to come together in a "same time, next year" group. They chose the frog as a mascot, since the frog is considered lucky in gambling in Las Vegas. They met for several years and did just that. Then things changed and the group became smaller. One person died and some could not make the annual visit.

However, three continued and I am one of them. We felt we needed a new name as the make-up of the group was different and it no longer centered itself in Las Vegas. It's a big commitment as the annual visit takes three days and three nights and it is spent like a slumber party. Each person is a therapist and it goes like this. Each person gets a whole day to talk about their year and share their feelings, highs, lows, dreams, relationships, fears, and victories. They then get feedback from the other two therapists. This has been going on for many years. Imagine the richness and power of this kind of sharing!

We named ourselves "The Giraffes" because giraffes have the biggest heart of any mammal, are risk takers that stick their necks out, and have great vision that allows them to look over most things.

We have seen each other through the beginning and ending of relationships, deaths, job changes, grief, the fun of travel, the writing of books, spirituality issues, children, grandchildren, and the changes that come with each new chapter of life.

I love being a giraffe.

LESSONS LEARNED

From this "same time next year" group, I learned trust, sisterhood, resolution, deep organic laughter, soft gentle tears, strength building, and spirituality. It is my sister group. I have learned that I am very rich to have these holy women to share my heart, feelings, and soul with.

Cancer, the Hard Word

"We must embrace pain and burn it as fuel for our journey."
—Kenji Miyazawa

It's always exciting to be part of an award ceremony. My role in this event was to give an achievement award to a friend in my field. The place was Walt Disney World; there was excitement in the air. Waking up the morning of the award ceremony, I got out of bed and put weight on my left foot. I felt sheer pain and knew something was wrong. Eventually, our hosts brought me a wheelchair, but the excitement was fading as the pain increased. I got through the ceremony sitting in the wheelchair.

Next I went to the airport, and instead of flying home to Las Vegas, I flew to Minnesota to go to the Mayo Clinic to see about the pain in my foot. They did some preliminary testing and soon, I was immersed in a battery of tests that brought me to my knees. The first thing they found was a breast tumor; a biopsy was scheduled for the next morning. The biopsy confirmed breast cancer and I was in shock. No one in my family had ever had cancer. The word penetrated to my core and I couldn't talk without crying. The doctors gave me a couple of days to decide on action.

I felt like I couldn't take a deep breath, like time was standing still. How could people go to restaurants and bus stops like nothing was happening? How could my life be on such a focus and on hold while the world was going about its business? All plans went on hold and I thought about how different today was from yesterday. Yesterday had plans, schedules, people, and a future. Being told I had cancer changed everything.

My daughter and her children flew in from Alaska, my Minnesota daughter and her children came, and my son sent pages and pages of research to help me make a decision about what to do. Within thirty-six hours, the decision was made: I would have a mastectomy and reconstruction in the same surgery and do it all at once.

The next day, we did it all. We rented a unit at the Mayo Clinic and went full steam ahead. Word traveled fast and the whole unit was filled with flowers and cards, and the energy from my family and friends brought me through. My office carried on by itself and I took the time to heal. A call came from Betty Ford to tell me her story and wish me well.

When it was over, there was the necessary five years of three-month check-ups, the adjusting to a new lifestyle and body, and the support that came from other breast cancer survivors. My oncologist told me at the end of the five years to consider myself as a thriver, not just a survivor. She told me to change my language to simply state that "I had a cancer once and I don't have it now. It's over." I have always seen it as one of the adventures that shaped who I am and not a disease that I have. I am cancer free.

Yet the memory of each step of that recovery is something that I keep. As I am writing this book, I found out that one of my neighbors just reached her five-year goal. While I don't know her well, I went to her and told her my story and we celebrated. Without many words, without a long-term relationship, she and I have a special connection. There are so many ways to become "soul sisters."

When this whole experience ended, the doctors found out that the original reason for coming to the Mayo Clinic turned out to be "a foot fracture." It probably saved my life.

LESSONS LEARNED

The biggest lesson right away was recognizing that I had courage and resilience. Once the shock of the diagnosis was over, determination set in and the next five years were committed to knowing myself and taking care of my needs the best I could. Living every day since that time as though I don't know how many days I have left is a wonderful way to live. A visit with cancer is not fun, but the lessons from it are invaluable.

Trip Around the World

"Those who do not travel do not have
many stories to tell."
—Unknown

It was 2001 and we were learning to take some time for ourselves. We both had "bucket lists" of where we wanted to go. Unfortunately, they did not look at all similar. We each wanted to go different places, so we kept postponing any major trip. Then one day in October 2011, a brochure for a trip around the world arrived in the mail. It had both our bucket list destinations on it. We read it, looked at each other, and said, "Let's do it!"

On February 2, 2012 we sailed out of Florida for a seventy-two-day world cruise. While an adventure of a lifetime, the voyage still had its risks: we'd be far away from our families for a very long time, what if there was an emergency? Also, with the political climate changing in some parts of the world, we felt some risk in terms of personal safety. Looking back now, however, it was one of the best choices and risks we ever took. We went everywhere we wanted to go and found places to which we would want to return, places to which we could no longer return because of political unrest, and places we would never have the energy to see again. It was a perfect trip with perfect timing both in the world and for us.

We had a small and cozy room. I took afghan blankets with us, so it felt like home immediately. We hung a giant map up on the wall so we could follow our progress. We hung a set of birds on a long string, so when we came home, we could hang the same ones at home to remember our adventures in faraway lands. They were beautiful cloth birds hung on a ribbon.

Good friends had given us envelopes to open on Valentine's Day, St. Patrick's Day, and other days of celebration, so it was like getting mail from home every week or so. We traveled to thirty-one ports in twenty-seven countries, plus had our time at sea. A few of the highlights follow.

We woke one night at 3:00 AM in Port Said, Egypt, to a loud, scraping sound, and the blast of a distress horn. We had crashed into another ship! Everyone was running in the halls heading toward their muster stations. Standing on deck in our safety vests for what seemed like hours, waiting to hear if we were going to abandon ship or if it was safe to stay aboard, was a real wake-up call in more than one sense. Finally, we were sent back to our rooms, and given an hour to change our clothes, grab our papers, IDs, and a pillow. We disembarked, and then boarded a bus for a thirteen-hour round-trip to the pyramids, not knowing whether our trip would continue. By this time it was about 8:00 AM.

By the time we returned, the $9 million repair had begun and it continued as we set sail that night, a bit uneasy. Some work was done on the ship, some was done by divers when we reached the next port. Part of the ship was closed off. The work continued for the two weeks left on our trip and by the time we reached Civitavecchia, Rome, the ship was fully repaired and ready to start another cruise. The cruise ship company handled it very well and never skipped a beat.

Another memory was tipping the waiter to not bring bread to our dinner table, but rather carrots, celery, and olives. We ate sugar-free desserts. We enjoyed everything else and didn't gain a pound. We walked on the many shore excursions we took, and the ship had a dedicated walking path and exercise classes.

We shared a private dinner with "Dr. Ruth" Westheimer, exercised with Jack LaLanne, and took cooking classes with the late Princess Diana's private chef, handwriting analysis classes, and many yoga and dance classes. A long cruise allows for lectures about each port before arriving, and I felt I had earned a master's degree in history by the time I came home. We saw, we listened, we experienced.

When it was time to disembark, we agreed we would be happy to do it all over again.

LESSONS LEARNED

I have volumes of photos and stories about what I learned in the twenty-seven countries we visited. But the biggest lesson of all was that we, once again, had seized the moment. If we had not been in the right emotional, physical or mental state, we might have never made such a big commitment. Timing was everything. When we learned about the trip, we explored the possibility and took action. There is not one regret about this trip.

We also learned that we loved being together for that period of time. We became very close soul mates.

Spa Experiences

*"The greatest gift a mother gives her family is a
commitment to her own self-care."*
—Cheryl Richardson

Time Out with Sharon

Many of the women who participated in Onsite programs in South Dakota told me, "We would just like to come spend some time with you informally." That led to the creation of the "Time Out for You with Sharon" program that ran for several years in the 1980's.

The weeklong program in the Black Hills included meditation in the morning and then hiking. Each day we had some services provided. We could choose between massages, yoga instruction, manicures, pedicures, facials, and more. At least twice a day we would gather in small groups and share stories.

The Lakota Sioux and many others consider the Black Hills to be sacred. We were lucky enough to have some Sioux women in our group and they brought great cultural richness.

Amazing lush green trees, brilliant "on fire" sunsets, yellow and promising sunrises, and the homemade "loving" food made every day feel magical. It felt nurturing, like having close sisters, and it was fun. Each night we would do something unusual. One night it was a stand-up comedy routine by one of our guests. Another night it was a sage burning and telling secrets. One night it was sharing our bucket lists. We would laugh, cry, think, hug, and feel loved.

National Institute of Fitness

After semi-retiring in the early nineties, I missed seeing the many women that I had become good friends with when we worked together. The idea of going to a spa together floated up and I did some research. There is quite a range of spas, from boot camps to elegant luxury. Boot camp sounded the best because there would be the side benefits of learning to eat well, learning to love exercise, and staying healthy.

I invited four of my friends to meet me in Las Vegas, and we drove to the National Institute of Fitness (NIF) in St. George, Utah. This two-hour car ride was anxious, exciting, and mysterious. None of us had ever been to a spa before. We stayed overnight in St. George because we needed to check in the next morning at 6:00 AM. It was a toss-and-turn night, and by 4:00 AM we were up and ready to go. We decided the night before that we better eat breakfast—who knew when we'd eat again? The only thing open at 5:00 AM was a Denny's restaurant we'd spotted the night before.

The uncertainty activated the scarcity principle in us. While it can play out in several ways, for us it meant we would never see real food again. That thinking steered the car right into Denny's parking lot. All of us, even though we were fairly healthy eaters, ordered eggs, bacon, toast, jelly, a cinnamon roll, juice, and several cups of coffee. Satisfied for the moment, we headed to NIF admissions.

We lived in geodesic domes and learned all the rules. I loved the wonderful pools and exercise rooms. It was a little short on pampering, but our excitement could not be contained. For me, the very best was learning to love walking. The walking tapes and the beautiful landscape of the red rock mountains were breathtaking. With the red mountains, blue sky, and plentiful black lava rock, it was a bit of heaven. I have continued my love of walking since that very first visit to NIF.

The food was vegan, and there were no snacks between meals and Spartan servings when we did eat. We made a commitment to the program that we would stick to the diet with no cheating. They kept coolers of cold, peeled hard potatoes in a little closet, and if you became seriously hungry, you could eat a cold potato. I actually learned to like them.

We did, however, cheat twice that first week. Once, we went into town and visited a bread store where they had one-inch sample cubes. We felt that wasn't really cheating because it wasn't eating—it was sampling. The olive crusty cube, the Parmesan cheese cube, and the dark rye cube held us over for the week. One other cheat was when we snuck out and went to a movie; five of us shared one small bag of popcorn. We each had one handful, eaten very slowly, one kernel at a time. We attended NIF annually for about four years and what I learned there has stayed with me.

Canyon Ranch

The next adventure was to the Canyon Ranch in Tucson, Arizona. My idea of going to a spa was to learn *how* to get healthy and fit. My eyes bulged in amazement upon arriving and seeing all the other attendees looking in perfect shape. Time for the black tights and loose baggy shirts for me. Food was more plentiful, but no one looked as if they had eaten in the last six months. Such beautifully toned bodies!

This was a great experience and I ended up visiting several times before starting to present workshops there. I gave a four-night lecture program. First night: Insight into Relationships, good crowd. Second night: Value of Humor and Laughter, good crowd. Third night: Recognizing When Drinking Too Much, five people. Fourth night: Sexuality, full room, filled hall, and asked to repeat the next day. I went several years and liked the Canyon Ranch.

Miraval Wellness Resort and Spa

My first visit to Miraval in Tucson happened because my husband was on the board of directors; we would stay there when he was attending board meetings. He sat on the board from day one and we've been going ever since.

Miraval captured my heart, body, and soul, right from the start. For years before those early visits, I had been a "consultant visitor" at the Phoenix Spa in Houston, Texas, the National Institute of Fitness (now Red Rock Spa), and Canyon Ranch. Being a consultant visitor at these spas and centers means that they are able to market my name and my books, and in turn I am their guest and do some presentations for them.

Each of them had gifts to offer, but Miraval was different. It was amazing and wonderful. It had such a component of healing of the body, mind, and soul. There was the challenge area, a climbing wall, swinging in the air, and balance programs. There were lectures and workshops on relevant topics, and an equine program that was very enlightening and enjoyable. Its programs on eating and food changed my diet forever. Then, sometimes best of all, were the spa treatments. Massages, wraps, facials: Miraval's consultants were the best and I've visited with most of them.

My contribution to Miraval was putting together the Wise Women programs, an evening "session of interest" for women. For fourteen years, Wise Women programs have taken place during the four-day package that I am a part of each May. We have experienced workshops on grief, transformation, loss, joy and play, change, relationships, and spirituality. Each year some of the original group from twenty years ago welcomes new women into our family group. These women are amazing sages.

It has become a "same time, next year" sort of group and we have seen each other through marriage, divorce, empty nests, new jobs, new careers, loss and grief, and many other subjects. It is a great comfort to know we are there for each other every year.

Perhaps that's why I named it the Wise Women group. It really is a shared wisdom time, and each woman brings her story and takes home the victories and wisdom of her chosen sisters. I continue my workshops at Miraval; this book was inspired by some of my experiences there. The spa experience is a "gift we give ourselves."

LESSONS LEARNED

Each spa story is special in its own way. The "Time Out for You" programs taught me how unique and fulfilling experience it is for women to come together to celebrate being women. It whet my desire to do some event like this at least once a year.

NIF was such a challenge. It felt like a regimen that was going to make me a better person—and it did. That was the beginning of my love of walking and exercise. On goes the headset, my mind becomes a haven of my special music, and these hours are mine.

Canyon Ranch was a time to look around and meet people who had made fitness and exercise an important part of each day. They taught me to take the time and "commit."

However, Miraval brought it all together and challenged my mind (classes, lectures), body (exercise, spa treatments, challenge course), and spirit (lectures, workshops, ambiance). On top of that, the Wise Women each bring their own gifts and are so willing to share. Miraval also offers all the consultants who are there to meet the needs of the attendees. Lessons abound. It's where I gave birth to the idea of writing this book.

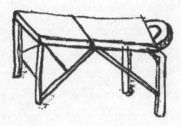

Chapter 8

FROM RESTLESS SEEKER TO SAGE

2012: Three Crises

"PTSD (post-traumatic stress disorder) is a
whole-body tragedy, an integral human event of enormous
proportions with massive repercussions."

—Susan Pease Banitt

My heart was heavy with restlessness at the start of 2012. The first decision was to be responsible and put my financial life in order. It was time to update my trust and leave my personal and professional life in good hands. I chose two trustees and three advisor trustees to manage my affairs after I die. Owning two companies at the same time, being an ongoing author, and managing a typical investment portfolio had made my financial life complicated.

To have started out with nothing and become financially independent required diligence and wisdom. I have hired good managers. But in May of 2012, events overtook all this care and diligence and rocked my stable existence.

In the middle of a three-day trust meeting in Las Vegas with four trustees in town for this meeting, I received a phone call: one of my daughters was in the hospital and seriously ill. If any of my children are in crisis, it becomes my first priority. We aborted our meeting.

I flew to Alaska immediately to be there if she needed anything. The idea of her being seriously ill was devastating. While there, I did the best I could in any way I could, as I would for any member of my family. It was three hard weeks until I came home.

While in Alaska, in my desire to help, I had overstepped some of my boundaries, had done too much, and in some ways was perceived as interfering. The fallout from realizing that was also devastating. It broke my heart for a long time. Shortly after arriving in Alaska, Joe became ill—very ill. We were stuck in a hotel room, and his only visits out were to urgent care where he was receiving ongoing care since we did not have a local doctor.

All that kept me going was the love and attention I was receiving from some of my grandchildren. They came by the hotel, visited with us, and let me know how much they appreciated and loved both of us. I will never forget that feeling of being loved.

We finally were able to leave Alaska, and we flew to Minnesota to the Mayo Clinic where Joe received care to help him recover from the seriousness of his illness in Alaska. Finally we flew back to Las Vegas.

While I was still in recovery from those experiences, my only sister called me several times to let me know that she was not well. As soon as Joe was strong enough to travel again, we went to Minnesota to see Sue, and spent some time together. While she looked good, visited with us, and shared her home, she seemed wistful and quiet. I pleaded with her to let us take her to the Mayo Clinic in Rochester, Minnesota and get some second opinions. She had several things going on; nothing seeming particularly advanced. But she refused. My sense was that she wasn't sharing everything. We returned to Las Vegas.

She called again and I pleaded with her again. She was quite short with me, saying that I was making too much of her malaise and that she wasn't going to the Mayo Clinic. I suggested we try another resource, but get some second opinions. She said no, that she trusted her local doctor. It didn't feel right to me.

The next week she called and we had words, but I told her we were coming to Minnesota anyway. It became clear to me that she perceived me more as a mother and that we were having mother/daughter issues. Sue was nine years younger and there was always a bit of tension. We had many good times, but it was not always easy. We went within two days.

By then, she had seen her doctor and was hospitalized in a small town three hours north of the Minneapolis Airport. We rented a car and went straight there. The report was already in; she had a large cancerous tumor and was seriously ill. With her permission, we had her discharged and drove her immediately to the Mayo Clinic, five hours away. On the way she told us, "I knew, I waited too long." She had been trying to get an appointment to see her doctor for a month.

By the time we arrived it was 10:00 PM, and we took her to the emergency room. After her examination, they ordered an ambulance to take her six blocks to the hospital where she was put on a palliative care/hospice floor. She underwent tests, but they determined it was too late to do any treatment. After two weeks, the hospital discharged her to home hospice, where she lived about three weeks.

This was one of the hardest times of my life. Joe was fragile from his illness and needed my help, my daughter was fragile from her illness and I prayed for her recovery, and my sister had died. I was going into caretaker stress mode. Everything became too much.

LESSONS LEARNED

Life as we know it can change dramatically and we can be brought to our knees in an instant. There are some circumstances that no amount of love, money, or dedication can change. I learned that no one is exempt from compounded loss. Navigating that loss hour by hour is all we can do. Somehow, learning that and knowing it at a deep level has made me a more accepting person. It happened in 2012 for me and also for some other people I love. Broken hearts abounded.

Trauma

*"The conflict between the will to deny horrible events
and the will to proclaim them aloud is the central
dialectic of psychological trauma."*

—Judith Lewis Herman

My life fell apart at this time. Having my daughter be so ill was devastating. She, her husband, and their five children were so far away, and they had such a different lifestyle in Alaska that is too harsh for me. I felt powerless to help them, and there were so many complications.

Learning to "let go and let God" was the only mantra that got me through that time. I respect their choices and have learned to let go, little by little. But though I love them all so much, there are limits to what we can give each other when we live so far apart.

Joe's health took a drastic turn that year, and we now live with that new normal. Age and illness are two factors that no one can control. Learning to live with limitations is another part of the letting-go process and another level of powerlessness.

The illness and death of my sister was life-changing for me. First of all, she was almost ten years younger, and in many ways, she was the healthiest in our family. She ate right, didn't drink or smoke, and she kept herself busy with her passions: her dogs, and an acre of flowers and yard. A social worker, she cherished her work and had many friends.

If someone who made all the right choices she'd made for self-care could be blindsided so fast by illness and early death, then no wonder I felt so hopeless and powerless.

I missed her smile, our talks, her goodness, our secrets, our love of perfume and funky clothes, and our talks about our family. She called me weekly and sometimes even today when I hear the phone ring, I can hear the words, "Hi, it's Sue."

With Joe's illness, my daughter's illness, and Sue's death, something inside me shifted. Everything mattered, and nothing mattered; there was so much to do, and nothing could be done. I wanted everything to change; I didn't have energy for anything. My belief in God was strong and I felt abandoned all at the same time. All that felt right was the need for change, as much change as possible.

We put the house in Las Vegas up for sale. We divested ourselves of most of what was in the house, personally and professionally, through consignment sales and giving as much of it away to recovery homes and domestic shelters as we could.

What we chose to keep were gifts, books, a few cherished art pieces, photos, two meditation rocking chairs, our clothes, a bedroom bench, and some kitchen items, the apple dishes in particular. My father had given them to my mother, and they were the only material possessions that she passed on to Sue and me. Growing up, we ate off those dishes every Sunday night; those dinners hold many of my happiest memories of home. (The full story of the dishes and their impact will come later.)

Many other articles from my childhood, from my grandma and my mother, had to go. This was all about moving forward and not looking backward.

Somewhere inside, there was a knowing that there needed to be space and time to make memories, not store them. I needed to focus on what was important and release what was not. It was time to unclutter my mind, my heart, my brain, and my soul.

What took me through the rest of 2012 and 2013 was the support of family and my friends and never-wavering faith.

LESSONS LEARNED

Trauma is the lesson that comes to us when suddenly our soul is seared with loss or pain. I learned that when several traumas are going on at the same time, we can be tested in ways we never thought we could survive. Trauma is a demanding teacher and I learned to live with it twenty-four hours a day with forty hours of things to do while my heart was breaking.

The help of friends and family was what got me through that time, along with my never-ending faith that God would be with me.

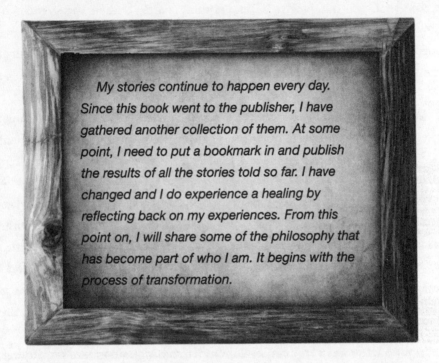

My stories continue to happen every day. Since this book went to the publisher, I have gathered another collection of them. At some point, I need to put a bookmark in and publish the results of all the stories told so far. I have changed and I do experience a healing by reflecting back on my experiences. From this point on, I will share some of the philosophy that has become part of who I am. It begins with the process of transformation.

Grief, Guilt, and Forgiveness

*"When we quit thinking primarily
about ourselves and our own self-preservation,
we undergo a truly heroic transformation
of consciousness."*
—Joseph Campbell

The trauma of experiencing such profound powerlessness over sickness and death brought me face-to-face with the grief and guilt that come with loss and imperfection—but also light the way to their resolution—and forgiveness. They are way stations on the way of the sage; natural, painful, but necessary steps to wisdom and freedom.

The Key to Inner Peace

None of us like to grieve, and yet it is through grief that we become strong and are able to go forward and make it through. The reason is that life is full of losses. Either we make peace with that fact and learn to survive loss, or we become emotionally crippled and unable to take action.

There are natural losses we all have: the loss of friends, a home, a pet, a love, an innocent childhood, being a teenager when we turn twenty, and free time. When we choose to parent, we experience the loss of children as they grow up and leave home. We can experience loss of health, loss of loved ones, and finally loss of life when our time on this earth is finished. These are all natural losses that most of us will experience.

Then there are catastrophic losses that only some will experience: the divorce of parents; our own divorce; loss of a job or career, health, or faculty; loss of hearing, sight, mobility, or memory. Some will lose hope, and others security of their person through assault, accident, or war.

All these losses are why we need to learn to live with as much balance and comfort in our lives as possible. We need to talk, share, experience, and integrate grief the best we can. We must recognize, process, and then express our grief.

Then, as difficult as it is, we must go through the grief the best we can. Sometimes we need professional help. Then we integrate that grief and loss into our lives and go on. We work toward a healing from grief on a regular basis.

We find some sense of tranquility. This is another word for serenity. It is the state of becoming calm, free from pain, loss, and guilt. It is "inner quiet."

Another great sage in my life was Anthony Padovano. At first I knew him through his writings and then we corresponded. His books brought me through some very difficult times. He wrote in his book, *Free to Be Faithful*, that it's no small thing to believe or have faith. He says there is a great deal of difference between loss, change, and transformation. Loss is a step backwards, change is an opportunity, but transformation is a step forward, according to Padovano. All of these things mean that someone has to give up something.

Loss is natural. We cannot hold on to all that we have to encounter in our lives. Change is also natural. We change from an infant to a child, a child to an adult, and from an adult to an elder. Every change requires a redefinition of ourselves. We are always surrendering. There is always a bit of pain when we change and lose something.

Intensive programs, reading books, or seeing a counselor can be a great help to many. But, at some point, everyone who's suffered a loss has to roll up his or her sleeves and pay attention to find peace, joy and wisdom.

From Anthony Padovano, I learned that the true sage is not a person who does what he or she has been told to do, but one who does what he or she must. It is not the one who remains committed to first commitments, but rather the one who remains committed to life at all costs. When we try to follow all the rules instead of our hearts, we may be taken into a life of mediocrity. The sage says, "No, I will follow my dreams."

Transformation, however, is about consciousness and bold decisions to change. It has nothing to do with time and age. It has everything to do with having values that must be acted upon. We embrace life, we look for meaning, and then when we find something that's meaningful, we embrace it—and redefine ourselves one more time.

A Waste of Time and Energy

"Guilt is not a response to anger. It is a response to one's own actions or lack of action," says Audre Lorde. Guilt is an absorbing feeling and brings about great distress. It's understandable to have regrets about things we have done; none of us is perfect, and we often wish we had done something differently.

Guilt is the feeling of being unworthy, wrong, stupid, and sorry. Sometimes it's alive and current. Sometimes, it's hidden in resentments and we hold it inside. If we do something that we feel guilty about, the fastest way to deal with it is to take action and rectify the situation. Yet sometimes we just don't want to face the issue. Then the guilt festers and eventually we have a collection of guilty actions for which we have neither apologized nor made amends.

This inaction turns into shame and we're stuck in resentment and negativity. At this point, we turn simple guilt into complicated shame, and that is both self-destructive and the cause of great problems in relationships.

In this state, we blame others for the way we feel, and there is a breakdown in relationships. A danger in turning guilt or anger in on oneself instead of expressing our true feelings is that, in this state of unworthiness, one stays stuck: in unfulfilling jobs, unhappy relationships, and punishing life situations.

Two of the most difficult relationships to navigate are the parent/child relationship and the partner relationship. This is because it is frequently necessary to protect and maintain one's power in these relationships.

It's hard to say "I'm sorry" when it's needed; it's also hard to be angry authentically and in a healthy way with each other. We need to know how to express anger in a constructive way.

Appropriate guilt makes us feel uncomfortable until we have made amends or restitution to the wronged person. To deny responsibility for hurting someone only reinforces guilt. The best way to relieve yourself is to accept the blame for your actions, apologize, and repair the damage. To break out of a pattern of a lifetime of guilt is difficult, but not nearly so difficult as continuing to live a guilt-ridden life. To get rid of unhealthy guilt:

- ★ Stop pretending that your feelings do not matter.
- ★ Be honest with your own needs. You are not obligated to meet the needs of others.
- ★ Believe in yourself just as you are.
- ★ Find your healthy anger and express it when you feel someone trying to make you feel guilty.

No one owns you, no matter what the relationship. You are not here on this Earth to fulfill the dreams, wants, or wishes of anyone else, whether parent, mate, child, or friends. You are also not responsible for protecting any other person from facing the consequences of their own actions or beliefs.

You are here to exist, to develop, and be responsible to and for yourself. In the big picture of things, it would be well if you also contributed to making this world a better place to be because you passed through it.

Forgiveness Is Freeing

*"Forgiveness says you are given another a chance
to make a new beginning."*
—Desmond Tutu

When we carry around hurts and old pain, we are the ones who are perpetuating how badly we feel. The person who we perceive hurt us, or the one we perceive made or makes us feel badly, is often not even aware we are troubled.

What is called for is to let it go and reclaim our own feeling good and happy. Easier said than done, you might say, and that is true. However, it is possible.

First, you need to acknowledge that you are hurt and upset. Either tell a trusted person or at least write it down and validate your own feelings.

Second, just feel the feelings. You cannot heal what you cannot feel. A good friend of mine, Mary Roush, wrote a book, *The First Eighty Years Are the Hardest: Feeling, Dealing, Healing*, in which she says the way to forgiveness and healing is to "Feel, deal and heal."

Once you have accepted the hurt and perceived injury and felt all of the feelings, the anger loses much of its power. Again, tell a trusted friend or write it down. You can destroy what you've written later.

Then *let it go*. Let yourself feel free of the particular situation and replace it with a feeling of having been heard. You can choose to stop letting it affect you. Fill your thoughts and your heart with a feeling of letting it go or releasing the anger and hurt.

Try to be part of a solution, not a keeper of the resentment, or someone who needs to fight back. Keep a vision in front of you of the new you: a person with hope and gratitude for what you do have. We never completely get over a serious hurt. We simply get through it. Pain can be a doorway to transformation. Parts of us can change. Facing our pain brings new lessons, lessons are knowledge, and lessons plus experience bring wisdom.

Forgiveness is more important to the one who forgives than it is to the one who is forgiven. Hasn't too much time been wasted on the bit of nothingness that brings about our anger and hurt? Is distance what we really want as we carry around our grudge? Forgiveness can actually put life back together again. It is proof that we have discovered a greater good. It is a mark of our own inner healing and self-knowledge. It shows what the forgiver actually values. It is such a relief to be one who forgives. When you forgive the past, you change the future.

The Courage to Change

"It's time to release our inner selves and surrender.
Powerlessness is not just for saints and mystical people.
It's true for all of us. Our part in the meaning and mystery of
life is to accept our powerlessness and accept we are
co-creators of destiny, not creators of destiny."
—Sharon Wegscheider-Cruse

I don't know what I would have done without the support of wonderful friends and family and my faith. It was their strength that helped me through the grief and guilt to forgiveness because I was no longer strong, in charge, or even very well. Sleep was disrupted, eating became a chore, and I lost thirty-five pounds. From the inside out, I knew powerlessness and loss. I was empty.

Always, I chose to live. Always, I knew I loved my family, and always, I counted on God's will for me. My daughter in Alaska was recovering from her illness, my daughter in Minnesota was there for my sister and helped her die, my brother was there for my sister and for me and he helped her die as well. Joe was there for me, and several friends helped to keep me going.

After being brought to my knees by multiple crises in just a four-month span, I truly came to understand deeply that many things are out of my control. That, in turn, made me much less hypervigilant and less prone to the worries that once haunted me. I have found a serenity and inner peace that is deep and constant. I need to cull the wisdom from all experience and let the rest go. At a deep level, I came to accept that I am in charge of very little. It is only me that can take care of me and it is only me that can manage my feelings.

It is important and there is a high value in being here for others, but only in ways that let them be them, and let me be me. Virginia Satir once taught me that my "yeses" would only have meaning if my "noes" had meaning. It has become much easier for me to say no without guilt and to say yes when I choose.

My self-care creates natural boundaries for me. My name on a certain time on the calendar means my time is booked—to read a book, go to a movie, or take a bath.

Sue gave me several meaningful gifts: a turquoise necklace, a coveted piece of pottery, a warm and cozy jacket, a book that I love, and hundreds of recipes. However, the greatest gift my sister gave me was the realization that we are all here today, but maybe not tomorrow. She went from diagnosis to death in five weeks. All we have is the now, and that's where I am choosing to live, with serenity and inner peace. As Sam Harris, author and philosopher, says, "You might as well enjoy now, because it is always now."

The support of friends and family, and the gifts that come from the discovery of powerlessness, gave me the courage to change again.

LESSONS LEARNED

Boundaries have always been a challenge for me. Finally, it's clear in abundant ways the need to have boundaries in more areas of my life. I know how to do it, but often take the easy way out. My lesson is to learn to be more self-nourishing.

Living Smaller

"Life will always intrude on our plans, decisions,
certainties, and fears. What can we do?
Look for the meaning and wisdom each time it happens."

—Sharon Wegscheider-Cruse

Almost immediately, I knew I had to move. Living in and loving Las Vegas had been easy. I had learned how to do travel and leisure, but eventually had too much of that—and too little community life. Deeply grateful for the friends I had made and fun we had, I was restless again, even though exhausted. The restlessness was a spiritual nudge for my soul. It was clear that what needed to change was me and my lifestyle.

Where to move? Joe had lived in Colorado and I had visited there many times because my son lived there. There was a part of me that wanted to go home to Minnesota, where I had lived the first forty years of my life. However, I knew I could not manage the long, gray winter months after living in the desert for twenty-two years.

Colorado, even in the winter, has sunshine most of the time. I wanted sun, light, and warmth. Also, I knew that I wanted an increasingly simple life. In turning my life and hope for recovery over to God, my philosophy became "Do one thing at a time and wait for spiritual direction."

The first thing was to go to Colorado after Sue died. We found a small condo in a very different kind of neighborhood. Instead of the very suburban life we had been living in a large house in a beautiful, quiet neighborhood, this two-bedroom condo on the outskirts of Boulder felt both urban and somehow rural. Every day, we are surrounded by life. We see horses, llamas, goats, and Black Angus cattle, as well as people riding bikes, walking, running, and just living their lives.

Boulder is jokingly called "The People's Republic of Boulder," and we join the many eclectic people who live in the area here. It is a university town and very intellectual. It has become a mecca for those that want to learn at all stages of life. We also have Naropa University (a Buddhist-inspired liberal arts college), very active fifty-five-plus groups, a focus on health, sage-ing communities etc. It is vibrant, different, generous, and interesting. While I don't live in Boulder itself, but in the county, I'm just a short drive from town and its many offerings. There is always a movie, workshop, music venue, street fair, farmers' market, or fair going on. Boulder County is also a mecca for bike riding, walking, exercise clubs, dog friendly venues, and all-around healthy living.

There is no way to hide in our small condo. It became a stepping-stone for leaping back into life; a much smaller life I have come to love. We had used every inch of space in our wonderful homes in Crestwood and Las Vegas for the lives we led then. Then our trip around the world had shown how unimportant space was; our cabin became our home while the world became our bigger home. After the crises, our lives were changing again—the urge to live smaller had already started with the first personal and professional decluttering in Las Vegas.

When I moved to Boulder, I inventoried my possessions and kept only what was useful, beautiful, or had spiritual energy tied to it. That ranges from a partly full bottle of my grandma's perfume, which brings an instant memory, to a painting done by a friend when I left Las Vegas, to a new reading chair. It's eclectic. When I recently did an insurance inventory of all my possessions, I was able to write a paragraph about every item in my home. It has relevance or it's not here. Life has become very simple in this move. As Peace Pilgrim says, "Unnecessary possessions are unnecessary burdens."

An emotional letting go mirrored this releasing of possessions and space. I made a commitment to let go of all my children and grandchildren. Letting go means accepting each of them and their own directions and not trying to influence or change anyone. This is especially hard since I want to be in their lives as much as I can. My learning is constant and difficult. They have their own lives to live. I am fortunate to have my son and his spouse live within walking distance. He attended college here and turned us on to this area. My daughters and grandchildren love where they live (Alaska and Minnesota), and I would never ask a child to move anywhere. They all make their own choices. They and their children come to visit us, and I cherish our time spent together.

It also meant letting go of the pain of losing Sue. Nothing will change the fact that Sue is dead. Yet I am choosing to remember as often as I can all the good times we had and how grateful I am that she was in my life for sixty-five years. I was near when she was born and I was near when she died. Whenever she has come to me in my dreams, she is happy and I choose to believe that she is.

The physical and emotional letting go made more space for experience. I am coming to believe that purpose comes from experience, not stuff. I began to focus on gratitude over ownership and consumption.

LESSONS LEARNED

I have learned that I need sunshine physically and for my soul. Colorado has an average of 300 sunshine days per year; that will take care of me in that regard.

Learning to live smaller has been a great lesson. For me, it needs to be beautiful or useful or I really do not need it. The world and the outside has become my home and my house is just to serve me. It needs to shelter me and comfort me. My biggest lesson is that I love small space.

I've also learned that when I have purpose and meaning in my life, it is sunshine for my soul. My lesson includes a different way of life so I have time and energy for my soul work "to be done." Living simply allows me the time, energy and space to really focus on what my "body, mind, and spirit" and have the time to pursue my dreams.

The Apple Dishes

*"Sharing tales of those we've lost is how we
keep from really losing them."*
—Mitch Albom

Even with all the letting go, there are some things I chose to keep that embody a cherished shared experience. Our apple dishes are one of those precious carriers of memories, a symbol that expresses how love can endure and inspire from generation to generation.

My mom and dad had very limited income when they started out. When the Franciscan Apple line of hand-painted pottery dinnerware was introduced in 1940, I was two years old. The dishes were pretty and my mom began to collect pieces here and there, and my dad would buy more pieces for her when he could so the set expanded over the years. I had to be older before I could wash and dry them because they were considered valuable.

We grew up with the dishes in a hutch, and no matter what was going on, we had a Sunday family dinner; it was the only time besides holidays that we used those special dishes. Those Sunday dinners were among my happiest times at home, with family and friends from near and far gathered around the table.

Ever since the fire that destroyed my dad's business in 1952, money had been tight, especially so in the months before he died in 1961. For years, Mom had really wanted stainless steel sinks. They were just coming in around that time and our kitchen sink was very worn out. She was very excited to have them installed in 1960. The sinks and the Franciscan Apple dishes were the house items she treasured. When I went to the bank to get my dad's safe deposit box, we discovered that he had been borrowing against the house to pay bills and feed his family. The house was now owned by the bank, and my mom had three months to vacate and leave behind her long-awaited sinks. She took the dishes.

My mom and sister soon moved and lived above my Uncle Cecil's store in Jasper, but there was no room for the dishes. They were stored in a friend's basement, which saved them when the store burned down, and for a second time my mother lost everything but the Franciscan Apple dishes. They stayed in that basement for years until my mother finally had an apartment in Little Falls, Minnesota, and later in Hastings, Minnesota, with enough space to hold them. Whenever we'd visit, we'd eat off those plates, and it was like all was better again. We enjoyed many meals at Mom's house on the "apple dishes," which survived two fires.

On one of my many visits to Little Falls when my mom was seriously ill, she told Sue and me to split the dishes. After she died, Sue said she would get the dishes to me. For whatever reason, Sue decided to keep them all. Mom and I had often talked of Sue and me passing them down to children and someday grandchildren. Sue knew the plan. She died without ever telling me why I did not get my share of the dishes. To her credit, one Christmas she gave me a serving piece. Another Christmas, she gave me another piece, but she never gave me my share. I received two pieces.

For years, I was deeply hurt. I started going to auction houses and to antique stores to start my own collection. I picked up a few plates over time, some cups and saucers, and one year for Christmas Joe bought me a bowl. I have used and treasured the pieces that I have and tried to connect with all the special childhood memories. I was sure that someday that wrong would be righted. When Sue died suddenly, I assumed that at this time, she would follow my mother's wishes. When she did not leave them to me in her will, instead leaving them to my daughter Sandy, I was stunned beyond belief and the old hurt was new again. It almost took my breath away. Sue obviously made a second decision that was not my mother's intent. It made me feel very sad.

Sandy, however, finished my mom's karmic wish. She knew what the dishes meant to me, and made arrangements immediately to have them driven from Minnesota to Colorado where they are now safely stored in my kitchen. In retrospect, I don't think Sue meant to hurt me; while I'll never know for certain, maybe she simply forgot the conversation. That is all in the past and the legacy of the dishes continues, once again making memories and serving the wishes of Anne Roelandt.

I have displayed them in a way that would make my mom proud and serve meals on them to all my own children and grandchildren and relatives and friends when they visit. The dishes have had homes all over Minnesota, from Jasper to Comfrey, back to Jasper again, then to Little Falls and Hastings; now they are in Colorado. They have seen joy and happiness and they have endured suffering and loss. I will take good care of them.

There are more of the apple dishes than any one person needs to use, so when I can no longer use them, I want them left to my brother and my children, and eventually to my grandchildren.

When the dishes are handed down, they will receive from their Grandma Anne the karma that comes with them that she wanted them to have. I trust that my brother and children will keep the love attached to them and keep the karma going to the great-grandchildren of Anne Roelandt, who didn't have much, but shared everything she had. I am happy to be a karmic link with these dishes and hope they will be as well.

Prayer Table

*"'Prayer' is called asking our Higher Power or
God for guidance. 'Meditation' is described as listening for
a response from our Higher Power or God."*

—Unknown

There is also one space we have kept wherever we have lived. Many years ago, one of my mentors, a true sage named Elaine Walker, told me about having a prayer table at her house and how she prayed each morning for her family and friends. It was immediately clear to me that this was an idea to copy.

Sometimes, the prayer table has been in a corner of our bedroom, and today it's in a small room of its own. When we worked in the Black Hills, it was in the angel room at our house so our group leaders could share this time with us when in town.

We have always had two rocking chairs and a table that holds water, plants, and our intentions. We use yellow sticky notes and on those are the names of people we are currently thinking about and praying for. There are countless meditation books, runes, medicine cards, and other prayer items that we use in our half-hour meditation each morning. We keep flowers, stained-glass window art, and candles handy, too. It's one of the best times of our day.

We also keep a coffeemaker and teapot and return to the room whenever we want to center ourselves or bring our memories of special people to the foreground. Prayer is an important part of my life and helps me feel that I can talk to God anytime I want and take some time to listen. What a way to become empowered! Believing in prayer gives me a respite from incessant fretting over minor everyday concerns and helps me through the big concerns. My prayer can be anything: a thought, a name, a request, or a conversation. There is nothing mysterious about prayer, unless we make it so.

How wonderful it is that our personal power comes from within, not from anywhere outside ourselves. Prayer—talking to God—and meditation—listening for an answer—help us to go within and search for our own truth rather than looking in some mysterious mystical self. Life becomes easier.

LESSONS LEARNED

First, we are connected to those we love through the prayer that goes out of our thoughts and our hearts. We have learned great compassion by being in the lives of so many we love.

Second, we are close to each other when we pray together. It's a bonding of trust, hope, and connection. We feel closer because of this half-hour or more each day.

Third, I have learned to go to this area when I am out of sorts, worried, or upset. Even the room helps me become more mindful just by being there.

Marine on St. Croix

"We must be willing to let go of the life we have planned
so as to have the life that is waiting for us."

—Joseph Campbell

Even though we let go of many cherished places and things, the memories we make in them and with them can make time stand still. One of them is the summer home we had in Minnesota when we lived in Las Vegas.

One day I happened to drive by a small, 128-year-old house in the enchanting town of Marine on St. Croix, population 600.

Driving through for the first time, it felt like a movie set out of the forties; picket fences, lilac trees, a lazy river running through the center of town, and an ice cream store called The Scoop. The first thing I noticed was that there were no franchises and the only grocery store was the General Store. Inside the grocery store was an old-fashioned meat market, a bakery in the basement, and a yummy-looking deli. We picked up sandwiches and continued our journey.

About eighty miles down the road, I decided I needed to live in that town. Turning around and driving back, it looked even more inviting. Driving around town, I saw the perfect house. Lilacs and hydrangeas were in bloom. The picket fence had a gate. I walked through and entered a comfortable and wonderful front porch. There was a new three-car garage out back. Two cars would fit in two bays; the third would be perfect for a tap dance studio. I bought it.

It was interesting to find out that this town was the prototype for Garrison Keillor's fictional Lake Wobegon, and he actually lived there for a while. I also discovered that the general store is Ralph's Pretty Good Grocery store, and that the characters that Sophia Loren and Walter Matthau played in

Grumpy Old Men were married in the little church across the street from our house. We spent six months out of the year there for seven years during our time in Las Vegas.

Our backyard served as a walkway for the plentiful deer in the area and became an early morning salad bar. I adjusted to enjoying the flowers when in bloom and then sacrificing many to the deer.

Each day I would take walks, including in the local cemetery. The locals had many stories about the graves, which were sort of a history of the town. On Memorial Day the townspeople would gather and walk to the cemetery. Large coffee urns and homemade goodies were placed every few grave sites. Someone from the school would read the names of any serviceman from this town who had been lost in the war. The bugles would play, and we would remember our loved ones with prayer.

On the Fourth of July, about 11:30 AM, everyone from near and far would line the main street of the two-block downtown. Each home would put a stand in their front yard and serve coffee, milk, Bloody Marys, and mimosas as everyone awaited the noon whistle, which blew at 12:00 PM every day. Right when the whistle blew, dozens of children, babies, and toddlers went down that stretch with their tricycles, bikes, wagons, and strollers decorated for the parade.

Following them was a parade with about eighty cleverly decorated floats peopled by politicians and participants done up in amusing outfits—all in red, white, and blue costumes. It was quite the day as picnics began happening all over town. We enjoyed seven Independence Days with all their festive flair.

All my children and grandchildren became an important part of our summers at Marine on St. Croix and we had several family reunions there. The children from Alaska would sometimes stay for a week or two; one year, we even opened up the house to have a special Christmas there. However, as we downsized and simplified in the wake of the health crises and my sister's death in 2012, the time came to sell that cherished summer home. It had brought us many great and joy-filled years. As you drive into the local cemetery and turn left, you'll see four plots that I own and will share among the family—and spend my eternity in one of them.

LESSONS LEARNED

I learned that we can make time stand still. There are places that each of us can find that bring us to our roots and that still exist. We can go back in time and find parts of ourselves. It may be a tree, a garden, a river, or a mountain. Wherever it is, it waits for our return, to know that we were on this Earth and fulfilled our time as a link in a chain. We all need to find that place.

Crisis and Caretaking, Again

"Physical strength is measured by what we can carry,
spiritual strength by what we can bear."
—Unknown

The move to Boulder in 2014 brought a welcome, if brief, respite from the trials of 2012 and 2013. Just two months after we settled in, Joe became ill again, even more gravely than he had been in Alaska.

Once more I was back into the role of caretaker, which I came to describe as a forty-hour job in a twenty-four hour time span. I wondered if I would ever feel rested again. Driving home from the hospital on empty streets at 2:00 AM, it seemed that the world was peaceful and quiet. Inside, my heart was crying and every fiber of my being was scared to death. Someone I loved very much was hanging on to life, and neither he nor I knew what tomorrow would bring. The powerlessness was visceral and yet most of what I felt was tired.

The hospital experience is different and the same everywhere. Waiting sucks energy and light from both patient and caregiver. Wondering and waiting. Wanting news and not wanting news. Hot and then cold. Some hospital staff are so helpful and some are so abrupt and quick. When someone is really nice, you feel cared for and you look for their name on the whiteboard, hoping they will be the one caring for your loved one.

I couldn't remember if I slept the night before in the hospital or did I go home? Can't remember. Promises to call people were vague. Did I call or not? Can't remember. Just wanting to sleep. Thinking is fuzzy. Walking into the house, it's as though nothing is happening—and nothing is. The mail hasn't been picked up, the dishwasher is empty, the house feels cold and empty.

Sleep comes very fast and then is interrupted by thoughts of getting back to the hospital, calls to make, and missing the one I love. This feeling is all too familiar; it's what I felt six months earlier when my sister died. Life is standing still and moving without choices all at the same time.

Later there are doctors' visits, tests to undergo, grocery shopping to do, bills to pay, driving, a home to maintain, friends' calls to answer, family to inform, meals to prepare. There is no time except for the essentials, yet caretakers do it. Why? Love, hope, need, affection, desperation, and goodness. Long days and short nights that go on, and on, and on. . . .

LESSONS LEARNED

For me, the physical aspects of being a caregiver were easier to manage than the psychological aspects. The worry about doing a good job, the powerlessness of watching someone suffer, and the fears of what was going to happen were overwhelming, going right to the core of my being.

Who Takes Care of the Caretaker?

"When I loved myself enough, I began leaving
whatever wasn't healthy. This meant people, jobs,
my own beliefs and habits—anything that kept me small.
My judgment called it disloyal.
Now I see it as self-loving."

—Kim McMillen

After four different types of caregiving in two years, I was depleted of energy and joy. There was always too much to do, nothing felt finished, there was no time for me, and I frequently felt sad. It was nobody's fault; it just was.

I thought of the people in my life going shopping, going out to lunch, attending conferences, going on vacation, and traveling. I yearned for time, freedom, and less worry. I saw people with fun hobbies and adventures. I was clearly going through a rough spell.

In looking closer at those around me, I also saw a family member who was working full time and with her husband caring for a child with special needs. This was going to be a permanent role. One of my girlfriends lost her son in a pedestrian accident and now is primary caretaker for her husband, who is quite ill. She does all this while volunteering to be a leader mentoring other women and bringing joy into their lives.

My good fortune is to know a man who is in a love relationship, has an important job as a hospice nurse, and still visits his mother, who has memory problems and needs quite a bit of care. He spends time with her every day. Three of my friends are facing cancer this year, and each of them has a family member who is holding their hand through the chemo, the radiation, and the surgery.

Who takes care of the caretaker? My conclusion is that the caretaker learns to measure time and energy, to put a bookmark in the caregiving somehow, to ask for help, and eventually to care for him or herself.

LESSONS LEARNED

I sought the help of two sages. One lives in another state and I went to him to gather wisdom. The other is here in my own area and I visit with her once a week. It clears my mind and comforts my soul to tell her my stories. Long walks with music level out the ups and downs; they are invigorating and sometimes meditative. I invite people to come into my space and enjoy holidays, play games, and break bread around a meal. Music, films, and performances take me to another place. I have created a meditation space in my home where peace and comfort are there for me each morning. My job is to take care of myself. It has been a slow and healing journey.

Reflections on
Family and Relationships

"The question is not, 'What do we want to know about people?'
It's, 'What do people want to tell about themselves?'"

—Mark Zuckerberg

It became clear that I owed my survival from the crises of 2012 through 2014 to the strength and support of family and friends. The loss of my sister and the threat of illness of my daughter as well as death of my soul mate led me to a slow awakening on the deepest level; I had known that relationships are the heart of life itself. They made me, and they saved me.

This recognition and acceptance made it easier to let go of the places and things that no longer served my connection to God or to the people I love and who love me. The letting go also opened the time and space to fully accept and appreciate the most important relationships in my life and what we have shared.

Telling one's story is personal and comes from a single perspective. One's closest relationships are intertwined with one's own story, and it's difficult not to tell their stories as well. In telling my story, great care and thought have gone into maintaining the privacy of each person, and letting them find the joy and satisfaction of telling their own stories from their perspective. There are no secrets or reasons to leave them out of most of my book other than granting them privacy. Included here is a thumbnail sketch of the most important people in my life.

My Children

"You can kiss your family and friends good-bye and
put miles between you, but at the same time, you carry them with
you in your heart, your mind, your stomach, because you do
not just live in a world, but a world lives in you."
—Frederick Buechner

During much of my career helping families heal, I was often asked about my own family. How did I protect them? One of the ways was by publicly saying and writing very little about them. There are, however, some things that can make them more real to the reader while still protecting their privacy.

I have three children: one son and two daughters. They have always been my first interest and greatest love. My children have always been and continue to be the most important contribution I have made to this world. Each is special in his and her own way; they mean the world to me.

I have chosen not to write much about them in my memoirs. My reason is that they are all individuals with lives and stories of their own for them to tell. All through my career I tried to keep them out of my stories and philosophy so they could have privacy. I just wanted to be their mom.

I have referred to them in the book as they have greatly influenced me. I am very proud of the person each has become. Our life together was full of chaos and rainbows, highlights and daily love.

As they've grown up, some of our interests have come closer together. Now we can share as friends as well as parent and child.

The early years were magical. Each time I gave birth, it was like the world expanded in permanent ways. Each child was planned for and wanted. When they finally made their way into the world, it was like a miracle. No mother can ever forget the softness of a baby's skin, the way their hair smells, and the anticipation of every change: smiling, turning over, walking, and talking.

I will always treasure that I took the time to be part of those early years. I sewed, made toys, fixed up their bedrooms, and rocked and read to them.

As they grew older, our home was always open to their friends. I still remember each of those friends, and each of my children has gone on to open their homes to friends as well.

They all excelled in school and became voracious readers and learners. Because of the delays in completing my education, seeing to it that they were educated was very important to me. Today they are all exceptional adults. Of course, that sounds like a mother's evaluation, but anyone who knows them would agree with me.

Rarely did I miss a parent/teacher meeting. While unheard of in those days, my belief was that the greatest teacher is experience. From first grade on, several times during the school year I presented a note to their teachers telling them my children needed a mental-health break and we were going on an experiential trip. It was never denied.

We traveled extensively, camping in Michigan, Wisconsin, northern Minnesota, and Iowa, and going to any other fun area where they could learn outside the classroom for a while. We didn't have money for airplane tickets, but we could load up our car. Later, we added airline trips.

My extended family also provided nourishment for all of us. My children loved going to the farm and seeing all of the animals. There was always good food and other children to get to know. My mother visited often and taught them to become good card players.

No matter how little money we had, we managed to get to Disneyland or Disney World very often. At first we camped and later graduated to hotels. There are hundreds of stories, from camping in Fort Wilderness and riding the monorail, to staying up late for fireworks.

We lived in several homes. We had started out in a brand-new home with forty full-grown trees. Along the way we lived in homes that reflected what was going on in our lives. No one ever complained; we made it work.

In the sixties, we lived in a house filled with the aroma of burning incense and had orange shag carpeting. Later our house was in an exclusive suburb of Minneapolis. We had a fire there when I vacuumed out the fireplace that still had burning embers. It was very scary for the kids as they came home from school and saw the fire trucks. In another house, when we were too poor for carpeting, I did the living room in giveaway carpeting squares from the carpet store. That was different.

We also enjoyed years of hosting foreign exchange students from Sweden, France, Mexico, Finland, Germany, and Japan. These were rich cultural experiences for my children. The exchange students would stay for fourteen months at a time.

Once we had a foster boy who was with us for almost three years. We tried to adopt him, but were unsuccessful. Once my son brought home a young homeless boy. He managed to hide and feed the boy in a closet for almost a week before he was discovered. Sadly, we had to return him to the authorities.[1] Our home was unorthodox and interesting.

When I went back to work, it all got harder; I felt overwhelmed much of the time. I was there most nights for dinner unless I was teaching a night class. We would usually play some kind of cards and watch one TV show. When they went to bed it became my study time until about 1:00 AM.

As they got older the travel part of my life took me away more evenings, and I will always regret that. Yet the dance between paying bills and having to be away was a difficult one. I don't know if I'd do it again, but I think we made the best of our circumstances.

They were wonderful children to raise and I now know I was a very good mother.

Today we play together, learn together, share love for their children and pets, laugh together, have a friendly give-and-take on politics, religion, and travel, etc. We've cooked together, suffered losses together, and cried together. The word that is important here is *together*.

They love people and pets, and are great parents, cooks, and professionals who have brought endless joy into my life. One of the best gifts they could

---

1 We had to agree to release and return each child to the system. It was part of the legal agreement. All we know about the homeless boy is that he went back to his home state. However, our foster son moved into the school district of one of my children and we met up with him again in seventh grade. He was doing so much better and it was great to reconnect with him.

have given is the spouse each has brought to our family circle. I love each of them. We may all have different names, but we are a loving family. Judging from the message below that they wrote for my sixtieth birthday, they agree.

Wow! 60 years! That's a lot of memories. As we celebrate your special day, let us share some of our memories of growing up with you.

We may not have eaten filet mignon, but we always had supper on the table. Remember "goulash"?

We may not have been driven around in a limousine, but we had a vehicle with character. Remember the van with the homemade curtains?

We may not have had European vacations on the Rhine, but we had fun family trips. Remember Disneyland and Taylor's Falls?

We may not have had our education at an exclusive, private prep school, but we had a Mom who was involved. Remember being a Room Mother, and all those parent/teacher conferences?

We may not have had bananas flambé for dessert, but we had yummy desserts. Remember chocolate chip cookies, and peanut butter bars?

We may not have gone to concerts at the New York Philharmonic or the Tabernacle Choir, but we had tons of school concerts. Remember Pat's band, Sandy's orchestra and Debbie's choir?

We may not have lived in the exclusive Kenwood neighborhood in a "Better Homes and Garden" house, but we had a comfortable, warm home . . . complete with personal touches. Remember the orange carpet, green curtain, and red velour dining room chairs? All in the same room?

We may not have hobnobbed with the Rockefellers and Kennedys, but our friends always felt welcome at our home. Remember Tootie, Sherry and Rhee?

We may not have had unlimited credit at FAO Schwarz, but we had creative home-made toys. Remember the book about the pickle and the onion, and the homemade Barbie doll mat? Cheyenne and Sierra are still playing with it!

No, the things we had may not have been perfect, but the love was. A family is like a quilt, stitched together with threads of love. Each year brings more memories, and strengthens the quilt more and more. Thank you for all the memories that have made our family quilt so strong. And thank you . . . in advance . . . for all the memories yet to come!

We love you, Mom!

My Grandchildren

"No legacy is so rich as honesty."
—William Shakespeare

One of my wishes is that my grandchildren will know me much better by reading this book. They know some of the stories that Grandma has told them, and my hope is that seeing my life in context, as honestly as I can tell it, will help them understand their own history and how we are all connected to one another.

There are seven of them. It's an amazing thing when your children have children. The cry of my first grandchild convinced me that my career needed to end. My children had given so much to me during my working years, and when I heard that first cry, I felt the need to give back. When my grandchildren were young they were a major part of my life.

The stories I could write have been written again and again by other grandparents. It's a love that equals the love of my children. Each grandchild is so very different that each could be the subject of a book.

Both my daughters were pregnant at the same time. Most of my friends were already grandparents and I was so eager. I knew it had to be the mother's decision, so I simply bought a rocking chair and rocked.

Then it happened. When the first grandchild was born, I was living in a different state. I flew to my daughter's side just before the due date and three weeks later was still waiting. Finally, on an October day, I sat in the waiting room and heard that first cry. It was like the cry of the ages. I heard the child, my daughter, myself, my mother, and my grandmother, and those who came before us all. It was the circle of life. I made a promise to myself: I would quit my job as soon as possible and be with my grandchildren as much as the mothers would let me. I had a grandson. Eight days later, I was in the delivery room with my other daughter and watched her give birth to my first grand-daughter. I pledged time to be with them. And I did. I stopped my career as soon as I could. Six months later I retired completely.

We bought a GMC van that held nine people. It also had a TV for the backseats. We would load up all seven grandchildren and one or both daughters and drove to vacations. I bought seven little pull suitcases and would pack them all in and away we'd go.

At our home, we built a huge sandbox, twelve feet by twelve feet, bought goats and horses, had parties, collected Disney classic movies, and even created a Disney World bedroom with Disney artifacts. They took turns sleeping in that room.

I could go on and on, but every grandparent knows the joy of being a grandparent.

Then circumstances took my youngest daughter, her husband, and her two little ones to Alaska. My heart came close to breaking. There were several times when the pain was raw and it seemed I would never recover. Time and visits helped. The two older boys and one girl came to visit and stay for extended periods. My heart sings and my gratitude is for the extended visits from grandchildren anytime.

To watch them grow up, even at a distance, filled my heart. Matthew, my first-born grandchild, told me when little that I could live with him when he got older. He would always have a little house on his property if I needed a house to live in.

Christopher liked to wear his shoes on the wrong feet. When I asked him to change them, he told me, "Grandma, some things aren't important." I never asked him to change again. That lesson has helped me in many ways.

Melanie has brought great joy to my life. One of my favorite stories happened when she was about four years old. She came out of the bathroom with her eyes rimmed in black marker pen. She had watched me apply eyeliner and wanted to be like Grandma. Luckily it did not get in her eyes—but it was not removable like makeup and took months to wear off.

Ryan taught me that food is to play with, not only to eat. He was a gentle soul as a child and remains a lovable man today. He loves pets and all animals and is determined to be there for them. I picture him at a zoo when he finishes college.

Cheyenne showed me her love for her pet when it was ill; it revealed the great dedication and perseverance she drew on to become a master dancer. She also has shown great independence and responsibility as she grows into a woman.

Sierra retaught me the joy of music. Listening to and watching her pursue that love is inspiring. Her music and singing is like listening to a seasoned Broadway star. She is joy-filled. She is also a grand baker.

Andrew and I have had to work to connect as he lives so far away. Yet any chance we get, we take it. In 2012 he helped me with many house projects in Alaska and we played well together in Hawaii. Another gentle soul, he has built his own computer.

Each deserves her or his own privacy; any reference is general in nature and meant to show how important they are to me. In some ways it has been easier to let go of my grandchildren than my children. That's because my children are such good parents and love them as I do.

My prayer is that each finds his or her place in this world and, with it, adventure, peace, and joy.

My oldest grandson has just married and brought a lovely great-granddaughter into our lives. God bless them all on their journey.

My Soul Mate

*"It is an absolute human certainty that no one can know his own
beauty or perceive a sense of his own worth until it has been reflected back
to him in the mirror of another loving, caring, human being."*

—John Joseph Powell

This is what I call Joe, my dearest and closest friend for thirty-plus years.
I am sure we have lived together in another life and will probably do so again.
We met, we talked, we connected, and we have loved.

My mother told me upon meeting Joe that he was the absolute right person because he was the only person who could talk about work, addiction, families, and personal growth as much as I could. She thought we were meant for each other.

Both of us were very strong people and had experienced hurt and emotional pain. There was no romantic nonsense in this possible coming together. We both were clear, vocal, and determined about our futures. We had many long discussions. There were obstacles, and we had to decide if we were willing to go through those obstacles.

We found a great therapist—a marriage and family counselor—in Palo Alto and had counseling for two years before coming together. He thought it would be a good idea to iron out any expectations and differences *before* we got married. Our careers had been and would continue to be separate. We had a legal prenuptial agreement as well as a spiritual and emotional commitment to be single entities and to create a partnership. We have stuck to that plan.

None of that has deterred us from being the best friends anyone could ever hope to be. We have traveled the world together, enjoyed other cultures. We traveled from Alaska to the Philippines; we traveled by air, ship, van, and train.

We have lived simple daily lives, opening the morning with coffee and prayer together, and ending the evening with a review of the best of the day, worst of the day, and the biggest surprise of the day.

Prayer time has been the glue that keeps us together and lets us keep our differences and clashes in perspective.

We've played hundreds of games and have cribbage buddies in many states, and cannot possibly count the movies we've seen.

We do our best to give safety, respect, joy, and comfort to each other. We have soothed each other in the face of loss and grief. We play together.

Joe has taught me the meaning of the words acceptance and patience. I'm a natural worrier, and he has slowed me down and given me peaceful times that have fed my soul and helped me take a broader view of myself and others. It seems we have spent a million rich hours talking, listening, and being there for each other. My life is rich beyond compare.

Memories of My Mom

*"You are my rainbow to keep. My eyes will always be
watching you, never will I lose sight of you."*

—Rick Riordan

In retrospect, my mom was a very lost child in her family. She was the one chosen to live with her grandma and care for her until she died. Her grandma died the week before I was born. I am the last to carry the name Rae, which is my middle name. The Rae family came from Scotland and is a very special one there with its own tartan. My mom gave up high school to take on this responsibility, and married my dad at seventeen.

She loved me and I always knew that. However, it was hard to connect with her because she had a way of making me feel inferior and guilty. It was hard for me to feel important.

She did leave me with some powerful memories, some good and some painful.

She would sit and rock me when I was a little girl and sing, "An Irish Lullaby."

When I wanted her to teach me to cook, she was always too busy and told me it was easier for her to do it alone.

She was very thoughtful and kind. On Christmas, while she wore an old and worn coat she bought my uncle, my dad's brother, a brand-new warm jacket.

She made two suppers each evening: one for Dad and us kids, and another for my uncle, who lived with us and covered for Dad at work at night. By serving two meals each night, we children could choose to eat at two separate times, depending on our schedules. My dad's business required late hours, and he and my uncle shared those responsibilities.

She hid a little blue metal can, with a butterfly on top, where she stored coins so if I really needed or wanted something, she would have the money for it.

She smoked, which I hated!

She drank alcohol, which I hated!

She gave back a beautiful satin nightgown to my dad on Christmas, saying she would have no place to wear it. He was crushed.

She was always kind to family, strangers, and visitors, providing food and hospitality.

She was depressed and sad much of the time.

She seemed very lonely.

I loved her.

Memories of My Dad

"Just one last chance, I wish I could hold you
and hug you. I miss you."
—Sharon Wegscheider-Cruse

Dad died at forty-six; I was twenty-three. My memories of him are also mixed and still quite clear.

I remember seeing him in his coffin, wearing the suit he had purchased for my wedding. He was handsome, but very cold as I kissed him goodbye.

Remembering him reading comic books with me and laughing about the characters.

Seeing him lying on the kitchen floor, passed out from drinking. I remember putting a pillow under his head and often one of my teddy bears in his arms.

His excitement buying me my first pair of earrings and bringing them to me after a trip.

Making homemade butter every Sunday morning.

Taking me in the family car in the snow and ice, and kindly and gently teaching me to drive.

Giving me his bottles of Orange Crush to "drink the top off" before he filled them with vodka whenever we went on a road trip.

He'd make me a fried-egg sandwich when I would come home from a date so I could tell him all about it.

As a young child, I used to comb and curl his hair while he took noon naps on the couch. Sometimes I'd forget to take out the pink foam curlers when he got up to go back to work. He would always laugh about that.

Being afraid when he started to drink and would get angry and swear.

I loved him.

Legacy Conflicts

"No love, no friendship, no family member can
cross the path of our destiny without
leaving a mark on it forever."
—Francois Mauriac

My Dad's Family

My paternal grandfather was a bootlegger; his product was potato alcohol. He was the father of seven; my dad was the youngest. I don't know much of his story, except that he owned large potato fields in Iowa and Minnesota, sold alcohol during Prohibition, and was an alcoholic himself. He also physically abused his wife and children.

When my dad was seven, his mother ran away and was not heard from again until he received a birthday card—on his thirty-seventh birthday. My dad was raised as an informal foster child on a farm in southern Minnesota.

I never met my grandfather. He died before my birth. As an adult, I met my grandmother one time before she died. My father forgave her for leaving and never said a bad word about his upbringing. The roots of this side of the family, the Roelandts, were in France and Belgium, and I connect to some customs in this family.

I only knew the extended family and I liked what I saw, but they mostly remained strangers to me. I only knew one of my aunts well and her name was Gertie. She was my godmother and lived in the same town. She remained close through my adult years until she died and was a positive influence in my life. She was the nursing home "prom queen" and rode in a parade when she was nearly ninety.

My Mom's Family

My maternal grandfather was a friend to me. He was sick a lot, but he told me stories and he liked to have me come visit. I went on bus rides with him to the doctor and loved him. His family's legacy was farming. They were simple people from Norway. He died when I was about fifteen.

My maternal grandmother was my source of family history, my support, and my role model all rolled into one. Memories include having an ice cream cone before dinner on a regular basis, the hundreds of doughnuts that she made and sold in her hometown, her laughter, her two special jewelry brooches she pinned on everything she wore. (I still wear them today.) We went on many train rides together. She came 200 miles to Minneapolis on a bus to see my children, her great-grandchildren. I remember sleeping in her bed with her and her sharing her life with me.

Her father and his four brothers had come from Scotland; they were the ones who developed the rock quarry in southern Minnesota that still produces jasper rock for building materials and jewelry. It was a rich and loving legacy, and this part of my family was the best family one could ever have.

My uncles and aunts from this family were all supportive teachers and role models. All of them were like second parents and I always felt like part of their family.

Visits with my grandma, who lived 100 miles away, could be one week or they could last three weeks. She would also invite my high school girlfriends and became close to many of them. This side of the family supported me always.

My Grandma's Funeral

"My grandma was a little bit parent, a little bit teacher,
a little bit best friend, and a little bit naughty."
—Sharon Wegscheider-Cruse

When my grandma died, I lost my sense of safety. She was always there for me. She had nineteen grandchildren, of which I was the eldest.

She played the organ in our church and led the choir. She was full of life and made each grandchild feel special. My childhood was often spent with her in her little apartment. We traveled together and she made me feel important.

Her funeral was a testimony to her life. She met with the Catholic priest the week before she died and made her own plans.

Her coffin was draped in a white cloth, as she felt she was being rebaptized into the life of the hereafter. It was an open coffin ceremony, and each of the nineteen grandchildren brought her a gift to put in her casket. As her oldest, I brought her a small bottle of Mogen David wine since she had a tiny glass each evening before bed. Another brought one of her homemade doughnuts; she'd made thousands in her lifetime. Someone brought a plant since she loved flowers, and another brought a teacup; she would have tea in the afternoons. Another brought a comb for her thick brown hair, another brought a rosary, and another even brought a small radio. She loved the radio news.

I had been estranged from one of my uncles. He felt I had abandoned the church by being divorced and should not partake in communion. It was an uncomfortable situation for the whole family, and everyone was anxious about what was going to happen at the service.

Unbeknownst to me, she had met with this uncle the week before she died and said he must forgive and allow me to follow my heart. As we approached the time of communion, the tension built. Then as the priest began communion, my uncle came over to my pew and put out his arm for me to hold and go up for communion.

There was a hushed feeling of relief and many tears when we realized that Grandma was still doing her healing work beyond her life. A healing in the whole family took place that day.

I still feel her presence in my heart and soul.

Dogs Are Important!

*"Until one has loved an animal, a part of
one's soul remains unawakened."*

—Anatole France

Dogs have played a very important role in my life. My childhood included Skeeter, a Chihuahua so tiny that she slept in a cake pan with a pillow. Then there was Pudgie, who would run a quarter mile to the drug store and sit on her hind legs and beg for an ice cream cone daily. My first adult family dog was Blackie: a puppy given to my son by his great-grandma, who said all children needed a dog. She didn't even ask if it was okay; she just showed up with the puppy.

Pepper was a story of her own. She was beloved by all our family except my first husband. He disliked her barking, and when she didn't change after the first year, he insisted I take her to the pound. Not wanting to just give her away without knowing who would love her, my three children and I took off in the car with Pepper and drove 100 miles to my hometown to find her a loving home.

This began three days of visiting families and friends to see who could give Pepper a good home—three days full of rejection. Reading the small-town newspaper, I saw an ad for giveaway dogs. With high hopes, we followed the directions to a farm outside town. Once there, the kids stayed in the car and I went to visit with the farm owners. I could hear other dogs barking and insisted on seeing the barn where the noise was coming from. Upon walking to the barn, with the farmer following me reluctantly, I opened the door. Inside there must have been over a hundred dogs tied to posts that were numbered. I swiftly walked back to my car and the kids and Pepper and I headed back to Minneapolis. We later found out that the farmer was doing some kind of research. I wrote a letter to the County Sheriff, but I do not know what ever happened.

At home, my husband insisted Pepper go to the pound and the next day I dropped her off. It was a Friday. The kids and I cried and cried, but he was insistent. Saturday night, at my bridge group, I mentioned that I was so hoping Pepper found a good family. Someone in the group laughed and said, "Old dogs don't go to families, they go to heaven" and that Pepper was probably already gone. I did not know that. The pound was closed until Monday and opened at 6:00 AM.

Sunday was a long day not knowing if Pepper was alive or dead. At 4:00 AM, the kids and I went to the pound and sat on the front steps, hoping someone would come in early. At 6:00 an attendant arrived. We pleaded our case, but he did not know if Pepper was alive or dead. We followed him past the many cages and all of a sudden we heard her familiar barking; she saw us before we saw her.

I paid fifty dollars to get her back and she ran into our hearts again. On the ride home, on the backseat, you could see her pride in knowing that she was loved and we had come for her. I simply told Tom she was staying and that was the end of that, barking or no barking. She lived happily with us for many years until she died sweetly of old age.

We also have stories about Snoopy, Mindy, Jake, Nicky, Scottie, Tasha, Trixie, Toby, and Ginger. And Daisy, BJ, Oreo, Jack, and Lucy. Each has tested our love, our loyalty, and our stamina. They have given their love, loyalty, faithfulness, and happiness in their own ways. Pets help shape who we become.

The current dog in my life is Molly, my son's dog. She is a piece of work and I love her. She and I have been dancing together since I moved to Colorado a couple of years ago. The dance is about whether or not she wants me in her space. She is protective of my son and not totally sure I should intrude.

However, she cares not whether I have combed my hair, added any make-up, or show up for walks in frayed and wrinkled clothes. Her tail wags the same way and she makes me feel noticed and cared about. She found the way straight to my heart. Her eyes show me her soul, and I get the feeling she is looking into mine. I'm sure others get that same feeling with their dogs, cats, horses, and other animals.

The part I love the best is when we meet other dogs and Molly just prances by, head held high on her leash, and gives off the feeling that she is loved, protecting me, and that we are family together. Sensing her pride, I hold my head high and walk with more of a prance myself.

Contentment in Colorado

"The person who tries to live alone will not succeed as
a human being. His heart withers if it does not answer another heart.
His mind shrinks away if he hears only the echoes of his own
thoughts and finds no other inspiration."

—Pearl S. Buck

The time in Colorado has given my soul the time it needed to rest and discover its next purpose. Our downsized life is perfect for the spirit to settle; small and cozy works for me. When I was young and home life seemed wonderful and chaotic at the same time, what I craved was a small space that was mine; perhaps it has been a safe place that I have sought all along.

For a while I wanted to be a nun. Later I realized that what I was craving was to have my own room, my own towel, and my own soap in a quiet, safe place. Later in my career, when living in hotels and motels was part of my busy work life, I had my own small safe place. It felt comfortable to me.

It seems that my soul has always craved a small, beautiful, quiet, and private space. There is a part of me that is very private, and I need private space and time. Fortunately, I live with someone that gives that to me when needed.

Much of my life has been lived in bigger homes with many people around. I have come to believe that the unpredictability of living in an alcoholic home led me to act in a circumspect way. It could be a wonderful gathering of family and friends, or it could erupt into an angry confrontation or inappropriate talk or behavior. It was always being on guard.

As my career flourished, my phone rang off the hook. Many people thought they were my best friend and there were times when I could get fifty calls between coming home from work and bedtime. Some were people who'd seen me at conferences, some had read my books and wanted counseling, some were peers in the field who just wanted to connect, and many others wanted referrals. Eventually, I went the route of unlisted, unpublished phone numbers. For a few years in the Black Hills, only our children had the home phone number. All calls went through my secretary at work.

To this day, it's rare for me to talk on the phone; I much prefer to do email. Phone calls too often interrupt something that is important to me. My good friends make appointments with me and wait until I am free for a face-to-face meeting. I find I have time for all those ways of connecting if I have fewer interruptions.

My time is simplified and streamlined. Learning to do only one thing at a time has given each thing I do its importance. If I give a party, then I give a party and enjoy doing each part of it. If I write a book, it becomes a focus. No more trying to do too many things at once. For me, multitasking does not work. When I am honest with myself, I can truly say, "been there, done that." I am no longer willing to stand in line for anything, including restaurants or concerts.

In Boulder, I feel I belong. Our favorite local restaurant is an example of feeling at home in a community. Some restaurants are just restaurants; others are community builders. Whether we stop in for a meal or a small plate, we see people from the neighborhood and people we know from other neighborhoods. They just come to visit. It's a grand meeting place. It's a local bistro with tables for four or six. It has a huge backyard behind it, so children can play while their parents dine. Its feels like home there.

Right from our first visit, we were welcomed by the best trained staff and an owner who wears sandals and Hawaiian shirts, brings his dog to work, and finds time to visit with regular customers for at least ten minutes. You get the feeling you are a guest in his home.

Only occasionally do I watch TV news. First of all, there isn't much good news and what is offered can be had on the Internet or radio. There's no need to be bombarded by dozens of repetitive newscasts. Also, I don't make time for anything violent or cruel. My time is precious and I treat it like money. Both money and time can bring me beauty, satisfaction, and freedom, but I get to choose.

The choices I made about which people to have in my life were not always easy ones, but they've brought me a wealth of love and strength that saved me when I was in turmoil. The choice to move to Boulder brought me to the time and place to simplify my soul.

With the events of the last few years, there has been a soul downsizing. What I've come to know is that I don't need to know anything more and if I do, it will present itself in ways that are simple and easily integrated.

This I call contentment with deep roots in acceptance and faith. And with it comes a new freedom—and courage—to choose that makes becoming a sage so satisfying.

LESSONS LEARNED

For some time, my soul has been restless for a safe place. My home in Las Vegas was magical, bright, and beautiful. But my soul was craving something different. I wanted to be outside, pet dogs, see children, walk through parks, stop and chat with neighbors.

My soul was crying out to belong to a neighborhood where there was lots of outdoor action. When I open my windows in the morning, I see runners, bicyclists, and dogs. If I look down the road, I see the edge of a golf course and occasionally a horse. If I go to the store, I'm likely to see cattle. I feel like I'm in the middle of life, and I've learned that that is where I want to be right now.

PART TWO

"It's good to be a seeker, but sooner or later
you have to be a finder. And then it is well to give
what you have found, a gift into the world
for whoever will accept it."

—Jonathan Livingston Seagull

My decision at this moment of my life is to put a bookmark in my stories and anticipate the next part of my life. I know there will be more stories, more lessons, and more to write about. A sage is one who gleans lessons from life experience. The rest of this book will be devoted to becoming and living as a sage. In other words, the time has come to share wisdom and take responsibility for being a sage.

Chapter 9

WHAT IS A SAGE?

"The popular mythology of creative genius depends
on beloved stereotypes of the artist in youth and old age:
the misunderstood upstart who forces us to see the world afresh;
and the revered sage who shows us depths of insight attainable
only through a lifetime of hard-won experience."

—Martin Filler

In the Introduction, I described a sage as a wise person who has learned to extract wisdom from experience and learned—sometimes with great difficulty—to choose to "let the experience go."

Years ago, I would hear professors and other leaders talk about so-and-so, referring to the person as "a wise old sage." Therefore, I often equated sages with wisdom. My visual picture was that male sages had long beards and sat in their man-cave and shared wisdom. They were like Native American male elders who smoked their pipes and told stories. Women sages had long white hair, wore beautiful long dresses, and also told stories.

More recently, I've read books that give me a bigger picture and a whole new way of looking at sages. Some of my favorite authors/sages and their books are George Valliant (*Aging Well*), Sara Lawrence Lightfoot (*The Third Chapter*), Jean Shinoda Bolen, MD (*Crones Don't Whine*), and Zalman Schachter-Shalomi (*From Age-ing to Sage-ing*).

Becoming a sage means to discover our connection to both the world we live in and our soul. It's listening to our personal truth and then sharing it.

Transformation Process

Somewhere, sometime in each person's life, there's a magic moment. It's when you take charge of who you are and you also let go of yourself at the same time. It's when you follow where your soul is taking you. Everything before that time was "chewing your cud." It's a good thing, but one never knows when the original transformation takes place. Do we know the exact moment a cucumber becomes a pickle, or when a caterpillar turns into a butterfly before it emerges from its cocoon? It's when the circumstances are right and there is a change that occurs. There is, however, an easy-to-understand cycle that we can learn to recognize.

In my life, there were many moments when there were "lessons learned." Some were easy lessons, and some were very hard. Each lesson trained me and prepared me for some big transformations in my life. Today, there are many parts of me that relate to the different lives I've led and the different experiences I've had, but in no way am I the same person as I was in other times of my life.

Age does play a factor in the life of a sage. The longer we live, the more experiences we have, and the more wisdom to be extracted from this experience. Yet, there are some very young people who are becoming early sages and there are many old people who have no idea what I'm talking about. Age is a factor, but not a determining factor.

The easy-to-work-with cycle of transformation looks like this:

1) Learn (take in more information)
2) Explore (take in more experiences)
3) Do (act on that learning and experience to transform)
4) Harvest (stop doing and just be and enjoy the fruits of your labor)

We repeat these cycles many times in our lives. Each time we transform, we become a somewhat new person. This usually happens when we stop doing what everyone expects us to do in a certain way. True transformation happens when you struggle with going against what is expected of you and follow your own intuition, soul, and knowing. When we go after what we want with passion, we get most of what we want.

Sages take their earned wisdom and manifest it in their outer worlds. The longer we live, the more wisdom we collect. Sometimes you'll hear someone say about a child or young person, "They have an old soul." That might be so true. Mothers have given birth to these people through physical pain, but these people have lived their lives in a way that has birthed their own emotional and spiritual transformation.

These are people who have found power and balance. This balance they epitomize is a balance of mind, body, and spirit. They innately know that when our thoughts, health, and values are in harmony, then the universal energy, which is available to all of us, is present. When this energy is released, so is our power.

Power is an interesting word and so often misunderstood. Power is not about control, nor is it dictatorial, nor is it unkind and judgmental. Power is energy that comes from within and unleashes confidence, competency, and compassion. It moves us to commitment and contribution.

Sages are powerful and wise. We recognize that power when we meet people who can:

★ Think clearly. They are not overwhelmed or scattered.

★ Work out problems. They don't stay stuck or confused.

★ Make decisions. They don't procrastinate or waver.

★ Make things happen. They know *someday* is *now*.

★ Influence events. They are leaders rather than followers.

★ Win the respect of others. They don't demand it.

★ Take charge of a situation. They don't wait needlessly.

★ Have a vision and carry it out. They don't accept current circumstances.

★ Be a force that unifies. They are creators, not destroyers.

★ What separates sages from other people is that they learn from their lessons, change unhealthy behaviors, and are willing to share how they do and have done that with others.

★ There is not a typical personality type associated with being a sage. Some may be very shy and only write, while some may be assertive (as opposed to aggressive) and love sharing in groups. Maybe they choose to share with their family. A true leader *inspires*; an aggressive leader *tries to change* others. There is a big difference in being a dictator and helping others find their voice.

Sages pursue happiness and pleasure and put themselves in places and situations in which they are likely to find true joy and satisfaction. They do so with ease and humor.

Sages deserve respect and attention from those they are connected to by blood or love. They take the wisdom they've learned through their life experiences and share it whenever asked. They leave a legacy for their families, their friends, and their world.

Sages experience mastery in their lives rather than remaining a seeker. Their power comes from within. Some call it a soul, a spirit, or an inner guide. It's the inner voice that helps us discover who we really are, what our purpose on this Earth is, and what kind of journey we want to take at this moment.

Basics of Wisdom

"Respond to every call that excites your spirit."

—Rumi

Each time we have an experience it comes with a message. Sometimes it's just a little bit of knowledge. Sometimes the knowledge has more grit and causes us to reflect and think about what is happening. We are never finished products; each time we add new learning to what we know, we become wiser.

Both crisis and victory are productive. It's not always a loss when we change. Sometimes victory changes us just as much as loss. That's how patience, strength, resilience, forgiveness, power, and wisdom come to us. Transformation is the path to becoming a sage.

Marcel Proust tells us, "We don't receive wisdom; we must discover it for ourselves after a journey that no one can take for us or spare us."

Adaptation and resilience happens throughout our whole life, and when we glean the learning from these experiences and adaptations, we become wise. That is why I believe that the harvesting time of our life just might be the most exciting and rewarding time.

We can set our intention to harvest at any age, but we best be well on our way by about sixty if we want plenty of time to harvest.

We Choose Our Journey

*"Becoming a sage is the reward given to those who
seek meaning and follow their inner guide.
They learn to live the double life.
They perform their work in the world and they
live in spiritual peace and contentment."*

—Sharon Wegscheider-Cruse

To begin to be a sage is to harvest the wisdom from our life experiences. The excitement of harvesting is that it's a different journey for each of us because we've all had different experiences. Once we harvest the wisdom from each experience, we are free. Our job goes from doing a karmic duty to being a role model for other searchers. It's enough to simply *be.* We become a human "being," rather than a human "doing." When we have meetings of sages, imagine the wisdom shared! That's why we must simplify our lives to make room for the sages to meet.

The older we get, the more meaningful our time and faith becomes. We get down to the essentials. As soon as your enlightenment and awareness tells you that you're ready, it's time to get serious about the rest of your life. When our spirituality grows up and we know we are part of something bigger, our daily duties and responsibilities are not enough. That's when our soul begins to direct our thoughts and actions.

Storytelling

It's important that our stories do not wither and die with us. Many families have untold secrets that hide pain, sorrow, and humiliation. Sometimes these stories are the missing chapters in understanding extended-family members, tradition, and expectation. Often psychological wounding gets passed from one generation to the next. Stoic silence and unshared stores are barriers to intimacy.

If we want to finish our karmic duty, it's often important to create a shared storyline and visions of the rest of our time together as a family. The more sharing that takes place, the easier it becomes to harvest our remaining time.

As we start harvesting, we stop asking questions about who we are, where we're going, and what we should be doing. We simply know that we are, we have experienced, we have explored, and we are gathering up our lessons and wisdom. There is nothing more to do. It's time to harvest our experience and tell our stories.

The Meaning of Harvesting

"A single conversation with a wise person
is better than ten years of study."

—Chinese Proverb

Life takes us through many stages and varied challenges. The skill is in knowing when and how to harvest our life.

Sometimes we expect too much too soon; sometimes we don't let nature take its course. The secret of a good life is to harvest each stage in its own time and not try to control outcomes. The harvest of our younger days is to learn and achieve; later the harvest is in exploring all that interests us.

This takes many years and leads us into the next phase, which is the time of our karmic duty. This is when we give back, do our jobs, give whenever and whatever we have to give to the world. Finally, we reach the age when all of our experiences are integrated and we find peace and serenity: this is the time of wisdom.

Now it's time to simplify your life and make a decision about what to keep and what to let go of. It becomes easier to say yes and no when you understand the shortness of our time on Earth. Choose where you want to spend your time, your money, and your energy.

The 2014 study conducted by the National Center for Health Statistics of the Centers for Disease Control and Prevention states that the average life span for men is seventy-six years; for women, eighty-one years.

That sounds so far away, but think about it: it's really not. Knowing that average means we could die earlier or later, we become aware of the shortness of life.

It's time to think seriously about becoming a sage and enjoying the harvest of your years to date.

Harvesting My Life

"Life doesn't get easier or more
forgiving; we get stronger
and more resilient."

—Steve Maraboli

What a gift I've been given to live this rich life with all of its ups and downs, losses and victories, and people with whom to share my stories. Writing this book has given me a new excitement, vision, and zest for life when the calendar tells me my life is growing shorter with each passing day.

Every day I feel grateful for being alive, mobile, and engaged with people and life itself. There are bumps and medical issues to mind, but there is so much to savor and enjoy. I choose to live in a way that allows me to harvest life. When we plant seeds, nourish them with water and food, then care for the seedling as it sprouts and grows, we look forward to harvesting that seed.

That's the way I see my life. When I was too young and unable to nourish the seed that was me, there were people who cared for me: my parents (who did the best they could), my extended family, teachers, and friends. I learned to pick up that responsibility and did my best to nourish myself. Gratitude toward those that gave to me awakened in me a desire to give to others.

I am grateful to have experienced so many things and have so many stories to tell. Over the years I have received countless letters and emails from people who have loved my stories and encouraged me to write this book.

My stories have enriched my life and made me happy and occasionally sad. I can say that I've had a full life, but I am in no hurry to leave it. I want this time of life that I am harvesting. It's when we no longer "do" that we are content to "be." That's a big word for me. Today I can say with great joy that I'm content. My restlessness is finally gone. It's time to harvest my relationships with my family, with my soul mate, with my friends, and with my professional life. Enough is enough and I have enough.

Instead of feeling diminished by age, I tend to feel an enlargement of mental life and emotional through recollection of memories and perspective. I have wisdom gleaned from a lifetime of experiences, and it provides me with daily appreciation of all that is going on around me. I no longer feel restless. I'm free to learn and explore when I choose, and to celebrate my stories. I've become a sage, no longer a seeker.

Sages Celebrate
What They've Done Right

"To live is to change, and to be perfect
is to have changed often."
—John Henry Newman

At times we all have a tendency to doubt ourselves and concentrate on mistakes or regrets. It's like there is a committee that lives in our head that is made up of all the people who have ever criticized us or found fault with us.

Some of the self-talk is subtle. Maybe we just didn't hear enough of what we did right. As a result we feel we are too tall, too short, too thin, too heavy, or our hair is too curly or too straight.

Maybe we grew up in a family of poverty or had too little, or maybe we grew in what Jessie H. O'Neill called "the golden ghetto." That means we've come from a wealthy family and don't know if people like us for who we are, or for what we have. Our head committee has so much to figure out.

Learning the difference between who we are (our self-worth), and what we do (our self-image), is important. We need to learn to love ourselves and choose people around that help support us with both self-worth and self-image.

Vein of Gold

Look for what author Mark Byron called the "vein of gold" that is in every rock. Each time we go through some of our history and find some of the good things we've done, our self-worth and self-esteem goes up a notch. We can keep a journal of only the things we celebrate about ourselves.

It's important to take some time and walk away from all our electronic work stations and toys and reflect on our lives and look for our veins of gold—look for the times when we did something right or made a difference in someone else's life—and give ourselves a pat on the back. Enjoy that reflection.

Inside each of us lives a unique and personal history and set of gifts. These are clues to unlocking the mystery of why we exist, why we are here, and what our destiny holds are inside of us. There is no one, no thing, and no magic to give meaning to our lives. We must mine that vein of gold ourselves.

Angels

Search your memory and find the people that were there for you. Name them and thank them. Next:

1) **Cut your losses.** Leave some people and situations behind. Someone or something might have served you at one time, but no longer does. We change, life changes, and our situations change. Keep no one who drains your energy.

2) **Build a new network.** Look for connection, excitement, and new people in your life. Build a "family of choice," a network of people who support and respect you.

3) **Choose from your family of origin those who love and support you with their actions.** Choose the ones who share similar philosophies.

4) **Celebrate all the angels who have been in your life.** It's fun to go back and find those who've made a difference to you and let them know. With today's instant access, you can find almost anyone. I've done this and it has brought me great joy. When the person is no longer alive or available, taking some time to look at old photos or even just to walk down your memory lane does much to increase your own self-worth by giving them some of your grateful thoughts. Angels are the people our Higher Power uses to bring new messages to others.

I have mentioned some of the many sages I have known throughout this book. I will mention a few more on the following pages.

Bob Subby, Spiritual Sage

"The illusions of childhood are necessary experiences:
a child should not be denied a balloon just because an adult
knows that sooner or later it will burst."

—Marcelene Cox

Bob is an amazing therapist and good friend. If he lived closer, I would like to be mentored by him more often. As it is, I seek him out when I am in his city; his wisdom touches my soul. On one visit, I was haunted and in some deep agony about some pain I perceived one of my children suffering. When they hurt, I hurt.

I bared my soul, and my inadequacies as a young parent, and my mistakes as my children grew. I was thinking my parenting wasn't the best. I so wanted to help and make things better. He let me cry and cry and finally, when the sobs subsided, I could breathe again.

He simply asked me about myself, and how I had learned my most important lessons. I reflected and shared some of my stories. He pointed out to me how much I developed resiliency and strength through some pretty tough times. I had to agree with him.

Then, holding my hands, he looked into my eyes and said, "How dare you think you should rob your children of the pain that would be their teacher? They deserve to learn in the same way you have—experience by experience."

He was right, I did not want my children to hurt or suffer any consequence if I could tell them the lesson and have them avoid learning it. I finally saw the folly of that kind of thinking.

Jerry Moe, Children's Sage

*"Good teaching is one-fourth preparation and
three-fourths pure theatre."*

—Gail Godwin

Jerry Moe is a gifted counselor who has worked in several children's programs. At the time of this writing, he is the Director of Children's Programs at the Hazelden/Betty Ford Center. I often refer to Jerry as the Pied Piper, which came from watching him in dozens of conference rooms and hotel lobbies. Without seeming to notice that anyone else is in the building, he will be walking, skipping, and laughing on his way, making his own path.

Behind him will be fifteen to fifty children all laughing or singing, having a grand time following him wherever he leads. One would imagine that this is a class, a course in humor, or an art forum. Little would one guess that these are children who have lived in alcoholic homes. They've known the loneliness, fear, and anger from a home where alcoholism has taken its toll.

These are very lucky children for two reasons. One reason is that they are in this program because one or two of their parents have sought recovery. Their recovery has helped them become more aware that their children need help as well.

And while their parents go to a long weekend retreat or seminar to enhance their recovery, Jerry is there to lead these children to their own recovery. He repeats his work over and over and has developed a single career of being there for these young children of alcoholics. I've sat in on many of his programs and am so happy that these children have this chance at such a young age.

Jerry has written many books and traveled the world delivering the same message: "Young one, this is not your fault and here is how you can take care of yourself." His is a mission of compassion.

Claudia Black,
Helping Professionals' Sage

"Every child deserves a champion—
an adult who will never give up on them,
who understands the power of connection, and
insists that they become the best that
they can possibly be."

—Rita Pierson

Some people are leaders and innovators, and some are needed as followers because the information is so important that it needs to be shared with large numbers of people. Claudia was and is that leader today. Coming from a family with a history of alcoholism, she led the way for many young children and adult children to find hope and healing.

Her iconic words, describing the family rules of dysfunctional families—"don't talk, don't trust, don't feel"—have helped countless people identify with her story and her wisdom. She's spent most of her adult life bringing her message of change and hope to people through workshops and speaking.

We became friends when we both served on the board of directors for the National Association for Children of Alcoholics. Her early book, *My Dad Loves Me, My Dad Has a Disease*, has brought many children to tears and then to comfort.

If Jerry Moe is the Pied Piper of children, Claudia and her countless training programs are the Pied Piper of the helping professionals who carry her work to people who need help and healing.

Larry Cumpston, My Financial Sage

*"A good financial plan is a road map that shows us exactly how
the choices we make today will affect our future."*

—Alexa Von Tobel

Larry will be surprised when he reads that I consider him a sage and that he is and has been an angel in my life for forty years.

This is how we met. When I started putting together Nurturing Networks, The Family Factory and The House, my financial life got complicated. I was still a single parent who needed help. While researching people who could help me, the same name kept coming up over and over.

So I made an interview appointment hoping he would take me on at a good price because I was just starting up. That didn't happen. He handed me over to a young man who was just starting out—apparently, I wasn't a big enough client. That young man was Larry Cumpston. It was one of the best things that ever happened to me.

Larry took an interest in my work and the fact that my girls were running a small distribution company. He liked the idea of helping families and jumped right on our team. He was my accountant, my advisor, my business manager, and my friend. Neither Onsite nor I would have made it without his professional help and personal support.

When it was time for me to leave Minnesota, there was no way I would leave Larry. It was the same when I left California, Rapid City, and Las Vegas. He's now part of my personal team and one of my trustees. He has taught me so much and I know I am safe with his wisdom and his integrity.

Larry has been and is a major sage for me. I don't make major financial moves without him. He's a friend to my whole family. I would like to think I am special to Larry, but then he's the kind of guy who makes everyone feel special.

Peter Alsop, My Second Musical Sage

"Musicians want to be the loud voice for so many quiet hearts."
—Billy Joel

When the titles of songs are as important as the musical sounds, you know you are working with someone special.

Peter came into our lives when Joe was depressed after a life-threatening accident. While he was recovering, I treated him to a conference on laughter and humor, thinking it would help the healing move more quickly, and it did.

He met Peter at a workshop and was enchanted. Joe came home and said I needed to meet this man as he would add so much to the Onsite programs. The minute I met him, he became part of our personal and professional lives.

Peter writes and performs music with a message, and is a highly trained and gifted songwriter. He has written more than 400 songs. More importantly, you want to follow him anywhere.

In our self-worth programs, we played his version of the song, "The Hug," and in our sexuality program, we played the song, "It's Only a Wee Wee, So What's the Big Deal?" In programs that dealt with illness and sorrow, we used "Nobody Knows for Sure," and for fun we sang "I Am a Pizza."

When our area had a serious town fire, Peter was at a program and volunteered to go downtown and play at the barricades to take people's minds off what was happening to their property. He talked a firefighter into taking us up on the truck to see if our home was still there. Peter came back six weeks later and did a benefit to raise money for our fire department—what a gift and what a sage he is.

Getting Rid of What Doesn't Matter

"Besides the noble art of getting things done,
there is the noble art of leaving things undone.
The wisdom of life consists in the
elimination of nonessentials."

—Lin Yutang

One of the blessings of becoming a sage is that you give up being the caretaker of unnecessary "stuff." Some of it's as minor as holiday decorations and some as major as your grandma's dining-room set.

When you are becoming a sage, you finally find the courage to look at your favorite business suit, your go-to black dress, the high heels that once made you look classy, and the designer dress you paid way too much for and feel like you need to keep it for whatever reason. But right now, none of it works.

You also can look with a discerning eye at all the cookbooks and magazine recipe clippings that you haven't used in years (you've already memorized the important ones). The same unsentimental eye can look at living room pillows that once brought color and imagination into your home and admit they are so out of date.

Finally accepting what doesn't matter anymore means changing behavior as well. Instead of turning on the TV to make sure we don't miss something, we punch the on-button on Bose and welcome the beautiful early morning with quiet and soothing music. Truly I do not miss all the smiling talking heads reporting the latest tragedy or crisis. My day starts serenely. Sages choose their settings. My space is much more simple and inviting without what has become unnecessary.

Every couple of weeks something is added, something that is temporary, but that brings newness and energy to my space. It may be fresh flowers, a book to read, or a special candle. When it's gone, it's replaced. William Morris, the famous nineteenth-century English textile designer, tells us, "Have nothing in your house that you do not know to be useful or believe to be beautiful." Clutter for me is anything that:

* Is not used regularly.
* Doesn't work.
* Looks ugly.
* Has unpleasant memories.
* Is dirty, broken, or uncomfortable.
* Is kept because it was expensive.
* Was a gift and has no use.
* Will be of use someday, maybe.

Sage Training

"Spirituality is a healthy relationship between body,
mind, and emotions that empowers choice,
responsibility, and change."

—Leo Booth

Sages tend to be ones who are called to be something larger than themselves. They're interested in others and the world. They give wisdom gained from their experience, are eager to share it, and are just as eager to hear someone else's wisdom. They're attentive to building a legacy that makes a difference to the world—their private world or the world in general.

They want to build this legacy and at the same time focus on inner reflection, role-modeling peace and serenity, and choosing to do more "being" and less "doing." This is an ongoing balancing act.

There have been many years of "doing" for me: getting an education, holding jobs, making a career, finding a mate, raising a family, and meeting family obligations.

It's hard to break old patterns of doing to the detriment of being. Too many commitments, too many activities, and too much energy spent doing things that otherwise would be good for us, such as exercising. In our programs at Onsite, we treated exercise addiction. People were surprised to find out they could numb out pain through excess exercise. The soul cries out for balance. Experience has shown me that balanced people produce balanced results.

Many therapists have a short list of "how to be balanced" as a person. These essentials definitely apply to being a sage.

1) Thirty minutes of meditation or prayer per day
2) Thirty minutes of exercise per day

3) Healthy eating
4) Expression of feelings
5) Sense of gratitude
6) Being able to forgive
7) Purpose
8) Some sense of spirituality

Sages Are You and Me

*"In times of change, learners inherit the earth;
while the learned find themselves beautifully equipped
to deal with a world that no longer exists."*
—Eric Hoffer

There are no graduate programs or workshops that teach you how to be a sage. There are no degrees or certifications. It's an inner knowing. It's when you are satisfied, content, and serene. It has nothing to do with action; it has to do with wisdom. Sages contribute to healing.

They have "a call" that comes from within. In busy lives, that call can be missed. It's the still small voice that gives us our truth. Each of us knows when truth is coming to us, and we need to match our actions to that truth. When our inner voice and our actions meet, we will find inner peace.

Sages are seekers of the truth, willing to share the wisdom from their experiences and able to find happiness in imperfection. Sages live through whatever life gives to them. Some great gifts are savored and many losses are struggled through. There are shifts in the hopes and plans for life. Sages are often weary and wistful, but rarely defeated. They have learned that life and the pursuit of happiness and fulfillment are a work in process.

They refuse to live in the invisible cage of existing. They want to connect, share, and tell their stories and truth. Sages know when they are on the right track and are recognizing their truth. Things get easier. There is more of a flow. If the same issues keep coming up over and over, then the path is not the truth. The truth does set one free and sages will find the authentic way. Repeating struggle is a good sign that the action or situation is not the true situation for the sage. They know when to give up, let go, and let something else happen.

Sages are spiritual. Not by long hours spent pursuing the study of spirituality. Nor by sitting through courses Spirit 101 and 102. It is not a mysterious process. It is as simple and as difficult as coming to know ourselves. Trust yourself enough to accept your own failures without disappointment. You take risks. Sometimes you win and sometimes you lose. But you keep trying. When you learn, explore, do, and harvest, you are living an enlightened life.

Problems for Wannabe Sages

It is only when you keep growing and changing that you come to the time when you can harvest.

There are many ways to get stuck in this process. There are those who get stuck in the student phase. They are always seeking more information, more knowledge. They get more and more certifications and degrees, and take more training and workshops. They are afraid to step out and produce.

The explorers get stuck in never reaching a satisfaction stage where they stick with something and make it work for them. They are the perfectionists who redo and redo and can't be satisfied with where they are at and what they know.

The doers get stuck and become the workaholics who can't slow down their inner selves long enough to find out who they are and what they want. They can't find their gifts because they don't take time to look. They are on to something more. Restlessness sets in when they are quiet. They have to be doing something.

Each phase of the cycle has potential for releasing personal power or producing a mode of being stuck. Harvest is given only to those who have gone to the dark and light places in themselves, forgiven themselves for any regrets or mistakes, made amends where they were needed, and turned over their fears and anxiety to the reality of a situation. They are able to know their own true self and know the gift of self-acceptance and self-satisfaction. It is a worthy goal.

Sage is a noun and an adjective; transformation is a process.
Sages are listeners. They distill what is important in a conversation. Sages
know they know and don't have to prove anything. Sages are quiet and

observant. Sages give short responses to complicated situations. They cut through the unnecessary. Sages are always learning. Sages have strong self-knowing and little ego.

This book celebrates many of the sages I've known. My life has been rich because I've had the chance to be mentored by, and learn from family therapy founder Virginia Satir, psychic Olga Worrell, healer Ram Dass (Richard Alpert when I knew him), Father Joe Martin, holy man Anthony Padovano, visionary Michael Murphy, and countless other teachers and healers. My good fortune also introduced me to some of the greatest teachers ever who changed my life in dramatic ways. They include Mrs. Margaret Mett, Mr. Bill Halos, my Uncle Vern, and so many others.

May you go on a search in your memory and find your stories and those who helped you become who you are today. It's a grand journey. I like me today. I am recapturing all of my dreams.

Transformation

*"It is a rare person who can pierce the veil between ordinary life,
consumed with matters of physical survival, and pursuit of the empowered
path of purpose and meaning unless he or she is motivated by a crisis.
Most often we require the failure of some system of power
that we rely on before we take action."*

—Caroline Myss

Experience. Glean wisdom. Transform. Change. *Transformation* can sound like a New-Age spiritual word and some will argue that it is. It's also just a word that states, "something has changed," in a small or major way. A cucumber becomes a pickle, a cocoon transforms into a butterfly, water freezes into ice. The original substance is still there, but with changing circumstances, a new form takes place.

That is true with us humans: we transform as we fully experience life. Let's look at the beliefs that we have, how they are formed, and how they can change.

1) First we have a belief. Maybe it came from our parents, our grandparents, school, friends, media, books, or churches—wherever.

2) Then we learn many things in life. Some things match our beliefs and other experiences might not support our beliefs.

3) Struggle and conflict can occur when our experience does not match our beliefs.

4) Choices need to be made. We need to bring our beliefs, new and old, to a balance and harmony.

5) Action needs to be taken. We then change in the process to acceptance of the old, modification of the old, or acceptance of the new.

6) The new belief or a modified belief is integrated and we have changed; we have transformed.

Our whole life is a series of transformations. If we make conscious choices and decisions early in life, we become wise with savoring our experiences.

Transforming people find the journey easier when they find sages and mentors along the way. We can learn from another's journey on the path. We live in a time when information and knowledge are exploding in all directions. That's why we need mentors and sages of all stripes: scientists, mystics, physicians, old people, children, youth, and psychics. We gather information from all those sources and then process that information through our "inner knowing and personal experience." *Knowledge plus personal experience equals wisdom.*

I love the word *masterpiece.* I am a masterpiece and you are a masterpiece. Who we've become is whomever we have invited into our lives. Transforming people live *in* the world and they live in the joy-filled and peaceful state of knowing why they do.

As people undergo transformations and move to different stages of spiritual consciousness, there is a tendency to feel as if they might be climbing higher and higher in consciousness. This is a myth; there is no higher and lower consciousness. There is simply consciousness—you are either conscious or unconscious. Conscious people will always be learning something new by simply "being."

Some talk of the God hole, the vague restlessness that many people feel. Never fear! That hole can be filled with great satisfaction, peace, and joy. If you keep striving for clarity, giving, loving, and understanding in your life, there will be no spiritual stagnation.

It's not a complicated journey. Don't waste time over past hurts and disappointments, and let go of resentments. Stay away from toxic people and situations. Pay attention to all of your experiential lessons and cherish your mentors and relationships. Keep going, keep asking questions, and keep loving. The restless space inside will be filled with purpose.

Choosing to Harvest

*"If you own your own story, you get
to write the ending."*

—Brené Brown

Anytime you want to become a sage, make the decision to harvest the wisdom you have accumulated all your life from the many experiences that have been your teachers.

Know that you are a link in a chain and all the stories and wisdom that are in you have the potential of being passed on to family, friends, and the world. Hopefully, we will each pick up that link, make it ours, and add it to the chain. Otherwise, our stories die with us.

You can become a sage anytime you choose to start. It's a joyous lifestyle. For those of us who are closer to the end of our lives than the beginning, our karmic work of living in the world is done. It's time to "be" in the world and let our wisdom be our contribution at this stage. Spiritual power is everywhere.

There may be some who prefer you don't develop your sage because they like your karmic output. When you are ready, you will teach them that your role has changed and you are going where the universe is taking you and that is your current mission. They, too, will get to be sages someday. Your karmic work is finished and the universe will support your new role.

Enjoy the journey. Let there be peace and gratitude within you. "Trust the process." Life is unfolding as it should. May you use all your gifts and then pass them on to those who come after you. That is your legacy. Find contentment and you will find wisdom. It's there for all of us.

The Now

"I am of the opinion that my life belongs to the whole community
and, as long as I live, it is my privilege to do for it whatever I can.
I want to be thoroughly used up when I die. For the harder I work, the
more I live. I rejoice in life for its own sake. Life is no 'brief candle' for me.
It is a sort of splendid torch which I've got hold of for the moment
and I want to make it burn as brightly as possible before
handing it on to future generations."

—George Bernard Shaw

Writing this book has been one of the greatest joys and struggles of my life. How much to write, what to say, and how to portray others, has been daunting. Thomas Campbell says, "To live in the hearts of the people we leave behind is not to die. I want to be remembered by family and friends." In addition to all the sages, mentors and wise people who have contributed to my life, there was Tony Bennett when he said, "It's very important to know what to leave out, thereby emphasizing what remains."

My admiration and support goes to all the sages who are willing to take on that role and bring their stories to those they love and with whom they feel a sense of connection. You are the only one who can tell your story. My hope is that you will consider sharing it. It is a wonderful legacy.

EPILOGUE

I am different now. Family and friends have told me I am different since I wrote this book.

It's made me think. Yes, I am different. It wouldn't be complete if I didn't share what that means. My intent in this book was to express my belief that "everyone has a story." There are upfront stories and we often know many of those stories about each other, and then there are the back stories. In the role of lecturer, keynote speaker, and workshop facilitator, I've often told my "upfront" stories, especially to make a point. In this book, I've shared many of my back stories, and that has changed the way I feel and the way I see myself. It's brought me great confidence and unparalleled joy.

I have a new, deeper compassion for myself that was not as clear to me before. There's a respect for all that I've done and accomplished. There is sadness for my losses and some holes in my soul. However, I celebrate my victories, heal from my grief, and have energy to go forward in a new and clear way.

In her letter, Virginia Satir wrote of me, "I know she knows what she knows, she knows when she doesn't know, and she is aware of the fact that she can be in the place where she doesn't know she doesn't know . . ." That's true. There is no way to know what my future will bring, but I am ready. My hope is to live many more years and enjoy my new clarity, but I am not afraid of the future and aging, including death. My stories to date have been told. I hope to build more memories and more stories.

Writing this book fulfilled my mission to inspire others to tell their stories. Write, verbalize, or record your stories. It does two great things. First, it's a freeing and powerful experience. It enriches not only your life but also the lives of your family, friends, and many you haven't even met. You make a difference. Do your best to not let your stories die or allow them to be forgotten. Bless the world with them.

ABOUT THE AUTHOR

Growing up as a shy child in an impoverished family afflicted by alcoholism, Sharon Wegscheider-Cruse has helped to redefine what healing means. She has built three successful corporations, written eighteen books that have been translated into thirteen languages, and brought hope and healing to millions as an author, counselor, trainer, consultant, lecturer, founding chairperson of the National Association of Children of Alcoholics, and founder of Onsite Workshops. Sharon has traveled the world and developed programs in the United States, Europe, Australia, and Canada, and has appeared on TV with Phil Donahue, Oprah Winfrey, and Larry King, as well as in multiple media events. At this time of her life, she is a sage who inspires others to become storytellers and harvest the richness of their own life stories.

She broke ground and fostered a movement with her books, *Another Chance: Hope and Health for the Alcoholic Family* and *Learning to Love Yourself: Finding Your Self-Worth*, and her film, *The Family Trap*. More than 50,000 people have been through her innovative programs at Onsite Workshops. From a wide vision that comes with living life to the fullest, she shares her story of finding inner peace and containment. Sharon loves her life with her soul mate, children, grandchildren, and friends. She lives in Boulder County, Colorado.